The Cranes are Flying

KINOfiles Film Companions
General Editor: Richard Taylor

Written for cineastes and students alike, KINOfiles are readable, authoritative, illustrated companion handbooks to the most important and interesting films to emerge from Russian cinema from its beginnings to the present. Each KINOfile investigates the production, context and reception of the film and the people who made it, and analyses the film itself and its place in Russian and World cinema. KINOfiles also include films of the other countries that once formed part of the Soviet Union, as well as works by émigré filmmakers working in the Russian tradition.

KINOfiles form a part of KINO: The Russian Cinema Series.

1 *The Battleship Potemkin*
   Richard Taylor

2 *The Man with the Movie Camera*
   Graham Roberts

3 *Burnt by the Sun*
   Birgit Beumers

4 *Repentance*
   Josephine Woll and Denise J. Youngblood

5 *Bed and Sofa*
   Julian Graffy

6 *Mirror*
   Natasha Synessios

7 *The Cranes are Flying*
   Josephine Woll

8 *Little Vera*
   Frank Beardow

9 *Ivan the Terrible*
   Joan Neuberger

10 *The End of St Petersburg*
   Vance Kepley, Jr

THE CRANES ARE FLYING

JOSEPHINE WOLL

KINOfiles Film Companion 7

I.B. TAURIS
LONDON · NEW YORK

Published in 2003 by I.B.Tauris & Co. Ltd
6 Salem Road, London W2 4BU
175 Fifth Avenue, New York NY 10010
www.ibtauris.com

In the United States of America and in Canada distributed by
St Martin's Press, 175 Fifth Avenue, New York NY 10010

Copyright © Josephine Woll, 2003

The right of Josephine Woll to be identified as the author of this work has been asserted by her in accordance with the Copyright, Designs and Patents Act, 1988.

All rights reserved. Except for brief quotations in a review, this book, or any part thereof, may not be reproduced, stored in or introduced into a retrieval system, or transmitted, in any form or by any means, electronic, mechanical, photocopying, recording or otherwise, without the prior written permission of the publisher.

ISBN 1 86064 504 6

A full CIP record for this book is available from the British Library
A full CIP record for this book is available from the Library of Congress

Library of Congress catalog card: available

Set in Monotype Calisto by Ewan Smith, London
Printed and bound in Great Britain by MPG Books Ltd, Bodmin

Contents

List of Illustrations	vi
Acknowledgements	vii
Note on Transliteration	viii
Production Credits	ix
1 Introduction	1
2 Context	4
3 Analysis	28
4 Reception	65
5 Aftermath	81
6 Conclusion	103
Further Reading	111

Illustrations

1 Mariutka and her White officer from *The Forty-first*. 13
2 Mark [Shvorin] playing piano among the decadent theater crowd in evacuation. 30
3 Boris [Batalov] embracing Veronika in the blackout scene. 32
4 Fiodor Ivanovich [Merkurev] learns of Mark's perfidy from Chernov [Kokovkin]. 35
5 Veronika [Samoilova] imagining her wedding. 39
6 Veronika's last happy smile as she opens her birthday present. 41
7 High-angled crane shot of Veronika and the anti-tank defenses ('porcupines'). 44
8 Boris, Veronika and Stepan [Zubkov] in the final moments before Stepan reveals that they've volunteered. 50
9 Boris and Veronika, separated by their private anxieties. 51
10 Irina [Kharitonova], the factory girl and Boris as he leaves the Borozdin apartment. 52
11 Veronika after the family flat is destroyed. 54
12 Boris's death. 56

The illustrations are reproduced by courtesy of the British Film Institute

Acknowledgments

I am grateful to Richard Taylor for his steady help, patience and support, and to Julian Graffy for the acute and sensitive intelligence with which he read and commented on earlier drafts of this book.

Note on Transliteration

Transliteration from the Cyrillic to the Latin alphabet is a perennial problem. I have used a modification of the Library of Congress system in the text. When a Russian name has a clear English version (e.g., Alexander), or when a Russian name has an accepted English spelling (e.g., Eisenstein), I use the English. When a Russian name ends in -ii or -yi, I use a single -y for a surname (e.g., Dostoevsky instead of Dostoevskii), a single -i for a first name (Iuri instead of Iurii). In Notes and Further Reading I adhere to the Library of Congress system.

Production Credits

Original Title: *Letiat zhuravli*
English Title: The Cranes are Flying
Release: 12 October 1957
Production: Mosfilm
Running Time: 97 minutes, black/white
Director: Mikhail Kalatozov
Based on: *Vechno zhivye* [Forever Alive], a play by Viktor Rozov
Screenplay: Viktor Rozov
Cinematography: Sergei Urusevsky
Music: Moisei Vainberg
Designer: Evgeni Svidetelev

Cast

Veronika	Tatiana Samoilova
Boris Borozdin	Alexei Batalov
Mark	Alexander Shvorin
Stepan	Valentin Zubkov
Dr Borozdin (Fiodor Ivanovich)	Vasili Merkurev
Irina	Svetlana Kharitonova
Grandmother	Antonina Bogdanova
Anna Mikhailovna	Ekaterina Kuprianova
Chernov	Boris Kokovkin
Volodia (soldier)	Konstantin Nikitin

1. Introduction

Every film buff knows early Soviet movies, the political and artistic classics of the 1920s directed by Eisenstein, Pudovkin, Dovzhenko and Vertov. But until recently only a handful of subsequent titles resonated among Western viewers. One of those is *The Cranes are Flying*.

Cranes enjoyed remarkable success by any standard, and astonishing international success for a Soviet film. After opening domestically in late 1957, *Cranes* quickly garnered awards at film festivals in Cannes, Locarno and Mexico, and received worldwide distribution. American audiences, conditioned by a decade of Cold War hostilities, still expected ideological certainties from Soviet films, and blinked with shock at the film's sympathetic portrait of human complexity. Western Europeans, though better informed about the changing Soviet cultural scene, did not anticipate the brilliant and highly individual style on screen before them. Even Eastern Europeans, compelled by self-interest to keep a close watch on developments within their powerful neighbor, reeled at the innovative, 'unsoviet' nature of *Cranes*.

Cranes amazed Soviet viewers no less than it did everyone else, although – having seen the range of Soviet films made in 1956 and 1957 – they understood more clearly the cinematic lineage of the film. For reasons discussed below (Chapter 2), Kremlin policies, film industry politics, changing social values and a metamorphosis in screen images and themes conspired to allow a group of individuals

2 The Cranes are Flying

– chief among them veteran director Mikhail Kalatozov and cinematographer Sergei Urusevsky – to make their picture the way they wanted. In *Cranes*, they fashioned a movie that rocked their society, forcing Soviet citizens to regard themselves and their history with different eyes, and influencing subsequent generations of film-makers. Along with Khrushchev's Secret Speech at the Twentieth Party Congress, the International Youth Festival of 1957, and Vladimir Dudintsev's novel *Not by Bread Alone*, *Cranes* became a symbol of the transformations in Soviet society designated as the 'thaw'.

Now, almost half a century later, and despite patent weaknesses, *Cranes* still moves audiences to laughter and to tears. The passion and compassion that permeate *Cranes*, its affecting relationships and dazzling camerawork, outweigh its melodramatic moments, overwrought musical score, and cardboard minor characters. For both historical and intrinsic artistic reasons, *Cranes* earns a place in the KINOfiles series. In this volume I hope to explain why.

Plot Synopsis

Boris Borozdin and Veronika are happily in love in June of 1941. When the Nazis invade the Soviet Union, Boris does not wait to be drafted; along with his best friend Stepan, he immediately volunteers for army service. His impatience to serve dismays both Veronika and his father, but the family – father Fiodor Ivanovich, sister Irina, cousin Mark, grandmother – gathers at the table to toast his imminent departure. They wait as long as they can for Veronika, but she, stopping to buy him some biscuits, arrives too late to join them. Boris's grandmother gives her the birthday gift Boris had ready, a toy squirrel ('Squirrel' is his pet name for her).

Veronika races to the designated departure site, but she fails to locate Boris, who for his part continually scans the crowds for his beloved until the volunteers march off. Thus the lovers have no chance to say goodbye, nor does Boris manage to write to Veronika from the army.

Months without word from Boris and a German bomb that kills her parents and destroys their apartment freeze Veronika into a state of emotional shock. The Borozdins take her in, and Fiodor Ivanovich, unaware that his nephew Mark has loved Veronika all along, entrusts her to his nephew's care. While Mark exploits Veronika's emotional vulnerability and rapes her, Boris – in the process of carrying a wounded fellow-soldier to safety – dies from a sniper's bullet. The family receives no word of his death.

Mark and Veronika marry. Along with Irina and Fiodor Ivanovich, both physicians, Mark and Veronika are evacuated from Moscow to Siberia. In the crowded barracks, where everyone waits for letters from their men, the other women envy Veronika for having her husband with her. But she never loves Mark and blames herself bitterly for betraying Boris. Mark proves to be corrupt as well as egotistical: a pianist who resents the war's interruption of his career, he spends his time socializing with a group of greedy and self-absorbed theater performers. He steals Veronika's toy squirrel, her only physical memento of Boris, supposedly to give to a sick child but actually as a birthday gift for one of the actresses.

Veronika, who helps out as a volunteer in the hospital, overhears Dr Borozdin speak harshly about faithless fiancées. He means only to comfort a wounded soldier, and does not have Veronika in mind, but her guilt so overwhelms her that she runs away, driven to the brink of suicide. At the last moment, she opts for life, rescuing herself by snatching out of the path of an oncoming truck a young orphan named Borka (the diminutive of Boris). The spell of passivity broken, she rejects Mark; so does Dr Borozdin, who learns that Mark has secretly obtained a fraudulent exemption from military service by exploiting his connection with his uncle.

Volodia, the soldier Boris was helping when he was shot, finds the Borozdin family in order to tell them about Boris's valor and death. Still, Veronika cannot bring herself to believe it as incontrovertible fact. When the war ends, a radiant Veronika joins the Moscow crowds welcoming the returning troops. Her arms full of flowers, once more pressing her way through throngs of people, she seeks Boris. Only when she finds Stepan, who confirms Boris's death, can Veronika relinquish her unreasoning hope in his survival and confront her own future.

2. Context

The Thaw in Politics and Culture

The 'thaw' conventionally denotes the inconsistent but prevailing relaxation in Soviet society that followed the death of Joseph Stalin in March 1953. It lasted until the mid-1960s, about a dozen years, mostly under the leadership of Nikita Khrushchev, First Secretary of the Communist Party (1953–64). Within weeks of Stalin's demise, writers openly rebuffed bureaucratic interference in the arts and defended their right to individual expression. But in the rigid hierarchy of the Soviet Union, such a radical change of direction required an official imprimatur.

That sanction came in late February 1956, on the final day of the Twentieth Congress of the Communist Party of the Soviet Union. Khrushchev delivered his major oration, asserting the Central Committee's 'resolute opposition' to the 'cult of personality alien to the spirit of Marxism-Leninism, which turns one or another leader into a miracle-performing hero and, at the same time, minimizes the role of the Party and the popular masses'.[1] He addressed his speech to the political elite; the population as a whole had no direct access to its text. Nevertheless, Party officials reiterated its themes in their own speeches, and editorials in all the main newspapers and magazines – including the chief film journal, *Iskusstvo kino* – repeated the crucial points. The sense of the speech, if not its actual words, permeated every level of Soviet life, from regional and local Party meetings to school auditoriums.

The Secret Speech resulted in a major reshuffle in the Party. More than a third of the Central Committee left, replaced by supporters of Khrushchev, and Khrushchev engineered the appointment of five new alternate members to the Presidium (including the man who later displaced him, Leonid Brezhnev). Across the country hundreds, perhaps thousands, of mini-Stalins – provincial Party secretaries, factory directors and local officials who had exercised their power with arbitrary and arrogant disdain for their subordinates, not to mention their constituencies – lost their positions in the wake of Khrushchev's excoriation of the Stalinist Cult of Personality.

Moreover, policy changes either explicitly countermanded or quietly permitted to dissipate the most egregious legacies of the Stalinist era. While Party policies did not shift suddenly, dramatically and in full public view after the congress, modifications incorporating the principles of Khrushchev's speech occurred in every area of life. Harsh laws pertaining to the status of workers, among others, eased significantly: compulsory transfer of workers, the ban on unauthorized job changes and the prosecution of absenteeism were all discontinued. 'Comrades' courts', instead of more punitive law courts, adjudicated breaches of labor discipline. The Party, hoping to solve persistently low agricultural productivity, allocated substantial resources for the cultivation of new farmland, and approved substantial price increases for foodstuffs: as a result, peasant incomes rose.

Much of the country's cultural and artistic elite welcomed the officially mandated changes, matching – indeed, often outpacing – them with a metamorphosis in societal norms and values. Khrushchev's speech at the Twentieth Party Congress and its after-effects empowered the passion for truth-telling that artists in every medium had expressed immediately after Stalin's death. They shared a common concern with and personal guilt for the moral compromises endemic to Soviet society. Evgeni Evtushenko's lengthy dramatic poem 'Zima Station', for instance, first published in October 1956, portrays a cynical writer, someone who has protected conventional wisdom instead of seeking truth, who now regrets saying 'what I should not have said' and failing to say 'what I should have said'.[2] That same autumn the prestigious monthly magazine *Novyi mir* serialized Vladimir Dudintsev's novel *Not by Bread Alone*, a stodgy text that appeared bold and dramatic because it caught the *Zeitgeist* so aptly. Its hero, the ethical inventor Lopatkin, tries to live up to the ideals he genuinely believes in; his opponent, an opportunistic and materialistic bureaucrat, plots and intrigues, obeys authority and ignores 'the ideals to which, in theory, [he is] dedicated'.[3]

All the arts felt the impact of the congress, cinema among them. The Party, promoting the industry's regeneration, had set ambitious target figures for film production: by 1960 the studios were expected to turn out one hundred and twenty films annually. It backed up its rhetoric with substantial financial resources, allocating large sums to construct new movie theaters and to renovate and modernize substandard equipment. Financial incentives – higher fees for authors, monetary awards for prize-winning films at an annual All-Union Film Festival first held in late June and early July of 1958 – replaced purely 'administrative' recognition.

The Party's plan called for seventy-five films in 1956, one-third of them from the nation's premier studio, Mosfilm, and another dozen from the number-two studio, Lenfilm. Most desirable were 'contemporary' heroes, preferably young ones, and celebrations of current success, especially on collective farms. Alternatively, film-makers could honor achievements of the past – the Bolshevik Revolution in particular, with its fortieth anniversary approaching – and anticipate those looming ahead, such as the Virgin Lands project, an agricultural scheme to create a huge new grain region in Kazakhstan and Siberia that would rely upon a massive voluntary labor force. The Party hoped that the Virgin Lands campaign would capture the popular imagination, and to an extent it did so, helped by films that emphasized the 'pioneer' element of the project.

Seventy-five films represented a substantial increase in the studios' output. At the time of Stalin's death, in March 1953, roughly a dozen studios produced a total of forty-four films, seventeen of them filmed versions of theater performances.[4] By 1956 and thereafter, Mosfilm remained the hub of the industry, but the republican studios had begun to revive, with Georgia and Ukraine the most active within the network of satellite studios.

The state controlled all the studios, from Moscow to Alma Ata, though the relevant oversight office varied: at different times, the Ministry of Cinema, the Ministry of Agitation and Propaganda, the Ministry of Culture. By the mid-1960s Goskino, the central state administrative body for cinema, supervised all studios: Mosfilm, Lenfilm, Gorky Studio, those in the republics and those that produced documentaries, educational films, popular science films, cartoons and children's films. Close ties bound the film industry bureaucracy to the political hierarchy. Right up until the demise of the Soviet Union, high-level film industry bureaucrats routinely had close connections with the Party Central Committee and often with the KGB. The Minister of Culture in 1955 reported directly to the Central Committee on the film industry, frequently basing his reports on information provided by in-house informants and anonymous letters.[5]

All the studios operated in essentially the same way. 'Script Boards' read and evaluated drafts of a scenario. Artistic councils [*khudsovety*], consisting of directors, editors, writers and other involved personnel, considered each script the Script Board passed. 'Creative units' [*tvorcheskie ob"edineniia*], the basic working teams, actually created the films. Within each team, the director made artistic decisions, the production manager handled business matters, editors worked together with writers and acted as censors, and a team *khudsovet* – critics, writers, actors, cameramen and others, plus at least one Party representative[6] – met to watch rushes, etc. Each finished film, once approved, received a classification category, upon which depended the number of authorized copies, whether copies would be in color or black-and-white, and where they would be shown: in the most desirable and centrally located first-run theaters or in outlying or older ones, in 'palaces of culture' operated by unions and other organizations, at film clubs.

After the Twentieth Party Congress the film studios had a considerably greater amount of creative space. The mandated growth in production necessitated a substantial increase in not just the number but also the variety of films produced. However unwillingly, the Party recognized that a measure of boldness might help artists 'accomplish the tasks' they were assigned. Disconcerting phrases – 'bold initiatives', 'artistic originality', security and 'tolerance' for the artist's individuality – began to appear in film commentary and even in official directives alongside more habitual negatives. Film-makers understood the import of the generalities: the kind of movies that had dominated the screen in the post-war period – musicals set in collective farms, historical hagiographies and costume dramas that portrayed the country as a static and unindividuated mass – had no place in the new order.[7]

What replaced them? Chiefly, films that attempted to depict reality, whether the reality of modern 'everyday life' or what film-makers perceived, however inaccurately, as the reality of the Soviet past. Furthermore, after years of imposed aesthetic constraints, film-makers took advantage of the state's gingerly tolerance for diversity – however limited – to explore a spectrum of artistic approaches. They could and did choose among a multiplicity of ways to portray objects and individuals on screen; they could and did shun the conventional paradigm of a single, predictable and judgmental authorial stance.

New physical types appeared on screen. The preternaturally sharp outlines of character and characterization typical for Stalinist cinema blurred and thickened into something closer to human beings, just as the irreproachably clear diction of actors slurred into something resembling normal speech. After a faltering start in 1954 and 1955, the movies of 1956 offered viewers a new vision of their history, their world and themselves. In retrospect, the early innovations appear minimal. At the time, however, 'the goals were more modest, the obstacles more fearsome'.[8]

For good reason. Apart from the fact that Stalin had been dead for only a few years, leaving a rooted legacy of fear, Khrushchev himself faced political opposition because of upheavals in Eastern Europe: strikes in Poland in June 1956, the Hungarian uprising five months later. Khrushchev's opponents blamed his conciliatory advances toward Yugoslavia's Tito and his de-Stalinization speech at the Twentieth Party Congress for lowering Soviet prestige and influence abroad, thus indirectly licencing the turmoil. By the end of 1956 international tensions and related domestic political skirmishes threatened the hopes kindled by Khrushchev's Secret Speech.

Six months of behind-the-scenes (or, more accurately, Kremlin walls) battles followed, culminating in a June 1957 meeting where the majority of the Politburo voted to oust him. Nevertheless, Khrushchev managed to defy his opponents' efforts to unseat him. He called a special session of the Central Committee and secured its virtually unanimous support. The Presidium and the Central Committee expelled Khrushchev's three most powerful rivals, and the wily First Secretary ruled once more.

Although *sub rosa*, these intramural tussles chilled the cultural atmosphere. Throughout the spring of 1957 liberals and conservatives duelled on the pages of most periodicals, among them *Iskusstvo kino*. Pleas for boldness, innovation and the elimination of bureaucratic foot-dragging coexisted with and increasingly surrendered to Cold War rhetoric and confrontational responses to foreign criticism. For much of 1957 and 1958, lackluster articles, pedestrian memoirs, archival documents and verbatim citations from or paraphrases of Party edicts dominated all major arts periodicals.

Artists balked, overtly or obliquely, at relinquishing the breathing space they had craved so desperately. Some manipulated history and literature, seemingly less perilous than fraught contemporary reality, to suit their present needs. In an essay on Stendhal, for instance, Ilia Ehrenburg invoked the French writer as a champion of artistic freedom, a man who 'hated despotism and despised servility'.[9] Readers embraced Ehrenburg's argument as a passionate defense of the artist's autonomy against the encroachments of tyranny and as a challenge to the spineless literary establishment – which demonstrated its pusillanimity by attacking Ehrenburg for his 'false, mediocre and stupid judgments about Stendhal'.[10]

In Grigori Kozintsev's cinematic adaptation of *Don Quixote* [Don Kikhot, 1957], Cervantes' mad knight confronts arbitrary and incomprehensibly cruel rulers. Only two years earlier, director Sergei Iutkevich had made of *Othello* a drama about faith that, though tested and shaken, ultimately survived. Kozintsev responded to changed circumstances and expressed his own bitterness by updating Cervantes' novel into a bleak assertion of the human need for faith, even when those in whom they believe – rulers and populace alike – prove entirely unworthy.

Khrushchev spelled out the new rules when he met with writers and artists in March and again in May 1957. Ominously, he compared the Soviet literary 'opposition' with the Petöfi circle, those Hungarian writers who had played a major role in the events leading up to the uprising. The warning was patent. All major arts publications reprinted the relevant comments. Editors everywhere recapitulated Khrushchev's main points: artistic obedience to the Party line, conformity to socialist realist patterns, ideological orthodoxy.

Anxiety mounted as infractions engendered consequences. The

10   The Cranes are Flying

State Institute for Cinematography [VGIK], for instance, the most prestigious film training center in the country, penalized students who had been too outspoken in their judgments and who had published an underground journal.[11] Khrushchev personally denounced Vladimir Dudintsev, author of *Not by Bread Alone*, for 'slandering' Soviet society, and he established a Union of Writers of the Russian Republic [RSFSR] as a conservative counterweight to the liberal and vocal Moscow writers' organization. The authorities postponed indefinitely a planned volume of Marina Tsvetaeva's poetry with an introduction by Ilia Ehrenburg.[12]

The state persuaded or coerced leading figures in the arts into retreating from the candor many of them had warmly welcomed after the Twentieth Party Congress. Most, though by no means all, complied. In the domain of cinema the hard evidence of 1957, 1958 and 1959 – reviews, articles and, above all, movies themselves – attests to a pattern of caution and retrenchment. Conservative views drowned out liberal ones; dogma replaced creative energy.

All the more shocking, then, to discover in that climate the first indisputable masterpiece of post-Stalin cinema, *The Cranes are Flying*, first released in the autumn of 1957. Yet *Cranes* was not *sui generis*; it had cinematic and thematic antecedents, some dating back to the 1920s, others of more recent, 'thaw' vintage. It united major thematic trends discernible in slightly earlier Soviet films, including the validation of private emotion over public commitment, the emphasis on 'ordinary' people, and the choice of the Second World War as a source of hero-images. Stylistically, it exploited the human diversity newly available to film-makers, and the potential expressiveness of a subjective camera. It was not the first film to privilege image over dialogue, nor the first to omit explicit authorial point-of-view, both characteristics of a number of films that preceded *Cranes*, though no other film combined them in quite the same way. Along with two or three movies about the Second World War (see Chapter 3), three films in particular paved the way for the exceptional achievement of *Cranes*: *Spring on Zarechnaia Street*, *The Forty-first* and *Pavel Korchagin*.

Cinematic Forebears

The question of heroism persistently preoccupied those who made, those who saw, and those who oversaw Soviet cinema. Audiences hungered for, and gratefully responded to, modest, unembellished film images of everyday life [*bytovaia zhizn'*]; such images satisfied the voracious appetite for 'truthful' art that was one of the most significant, if only partly realized, achievements of the thaw. But film-makers had to satisfy their bosses as well as their audiences (not to mention themselves), and the relationship between heroism and everyday life consistently presented a stumbling block. Mandarins in the Ministry of Culture and in their own studios urged scriptwriters and directors to represent the lives of ordinary men and women in typical Soviet milieus. At the same time, artists were exhorted to place individual concerns within a broader social context, imparting to or extrapolating from them a larger significance. Otherwise they 'trivialized' the social dimension of particular lives.

This explains the mixture of warmth and unease that greeted Marlen Khutsiev and Felix Mironer's *Spring on Zarechnaia Street*, perhaps the most important film released in 1956. The film, set in the present, abounds in authentic 'signs of the times', from the pre-war workers' settlement, muddy streets of little houses surrounded by crooked fences, to the modest interiors made distinctive by plants and knick-knacks. The faces are attractive but hardly glamorous; the young workers gulp down foaming (and quite controversial!) mugs of beer when their shift ends. Khutsiev and Mironer sought their heroes 'not in the center, not in the capital, not in offices with nameplates on the doors ... but in the very heart of life ... [they] felt obliged to tell people the truth about themselves and their lives, even if initially a rather inconsequential and private truth about their personal human relationships'.[13]

Spring takes as its model the standard Soviet 're-education film' that trumpets the reformative potential of labor, or its individual representatives, but the film is far more ambiguous than its traditional prototype. Although the 'concept of totally remaking human beings'[14] continued to pervade Soviet life, Khutsiev and Mironer refused to create a model hero (though he is a worker) or a model heroine (though she is a teacher). Neither protagonist can be slotted into neat categories; neither can easily be judged, since good and bad qualities, 'ours' and 'alien', coexist within them. Like other heroes and heroines of 1956 movies, the protagonists of *Spring* are emotionally and psychologically relatively complex. While still demonstrably 'positive', they no longer function as unambiguous role models, nor are their opponents instantly identifiable as villains.

Some months earlier, in *The Forty-first*, Grigori Chukhrai had thickened the simplicities of a Civil War melodrama in much the same way. For his first feature film Chukhrai proposed a remake of a Soviet silent directed by Iakov Protazanov in 1927. *The Forty-first* portrays Mariutka, a Red Army sharpshooter who guards a captured officer of the opposing White Army. They become stranded on a desert island, and fall in love. Eventually a boat carrying Whites nears the shore and the officer runs toward them. Mariutka snatches up her rifle, takes aim and shoots her lover, thus claiming her forty-first victim.

Chukhrai and his cameraman Sergei Urusevsky – soon to collaborate with Kalatozov on *Cranes* – used color stock to film Mariutka and her blue-eyed lover's idyll with such lyricism that the lovers' passion and tenderness enjoy parity with, if not indeed primacy over, any political commitment. Isolation permits revolutionary loyalty to take a back seat to love. 'Red soldier' and 'White officer', 'escort' and 'prisoner' become, simply, She and He, Eve and Adam. Their autonomous and elemental love breaches conventional Soviet film presentations of love as constancy, as mutual support, as friendship. Golden sand and golden skin, turquoise sea and azure eyes form a visual alliance of nature and love. Love rules unchallenged only in the unpeopled world of nature, however; there, it arrogates to itself such classic symbols of the revolution as the raging storm. When the human world impinges, it destroys that Eden just as inevitably as Mariutka's gun kills her lover.

Much of the power of *The Forty-first* derives from two of Urusevsky's many gifts: his extraordinary ability to endow landscape with emotional content, so that the desert itself, though nearly fatal to the Red regiment that traverses it, is sensual and velvety; and his loving, almost caressing homage to the human body in the second half of the film. Earlier, as the Reds cross the Karakum desert, they are muffled in their uniforms and boots. Mariutka, the only woman,

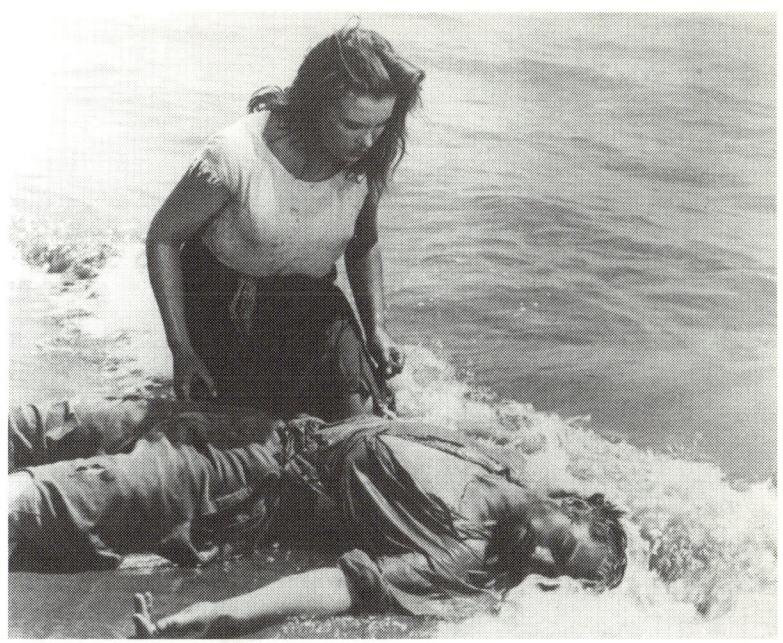

1. Mariutka and her White officer from *The Forty-first*.

is deliberately desexed. Like Nonna Mordiukova's Red Army commander in Alexander Askoldov's 1967 *The Commissar*, Mariutka's long hair is tucked away under a fur hat; an overcoat sheathes her body. When the soldiers finally reach the dazzling Aral Sea, only their faces reveal their ecstasy, as if they have no bodies. The Kazakh natives who help them are the same. The women wear ornate and colorful clothing, but the only females shown in close-up are presexual: 'She's just a child,' says Mariutka about one of them, 'not a girl.'

By contrast, when Mariutka and her White prisoner are shipwrecked on their island, Urusevsky shoots their bodies as extensions of nature. Warm firelight flickers on his lithe muscles; her sleeve falls back to reveal the vulnerability of her upper arm, her skirt barely conceals a rounded thigh and hip. When he tells the story of Robinson Crusoe and Friday to his rapt audience of one, director and cameraman construct out of image and music a wordless montage in which hair, lips and skin have particular beauty. Urusevsky's camera persuades us that their love, grounded in exquisitely rendered physical reality, is genuine, although the dialogue (Grigori Koltunov's script, based on Boris Lavreniov's 1924 story of the same name) is more problematic: the lovers argue politics more ardently than they exchange words of love.

The Forty-first exemplifies a central paradox of the thaw: a profound hunger for personal freedom that coexisted with and contradicted an equally profound belief in the 'collectivist divinity', even though the belief denies the yearned-for freedom.[15] Mariutka fulfills her revolutionary duty, but the final close-up reveals her anguish. She holds her dead lover in her arms, embracing him and weeping; the rifle lies forgotten on the sand. Despairing faith and doomed love collide.

This same paradox distinguishes another thaw adaptation of a classic of socialist realist fiction, *Pavel Korchagin*. Two young collaborators, Alexander Alov and Vladimir Naumov, had debuted two years earlier with *Restless Youth* [Trevozhnaia molodost'], a film enshrining Komsomol (Young Communist League) heroes. With *Pavel Korchagin* they challenged their own earlier naïveté, as well as deliberately stripping away any hint of euphemism in their portrayal of a squalid, disease-ridden and hunger-plagued Civil War-era reality, and were sharply criticized for it.

In the original novel, Nikolai Ostrovsky's *How the Steel was Tempered* (1932–34), Pavel Korchagin commits himself heart and soul to revolution. He dedicates all of his passion to it; he suffers irreparable physical damage because of it. Throughout all his trials his overriding concern remains how he can best serve the Bolshevik cause.

Korchagin belongs to the venerable Soviet pantheon of revolutionaries who willingly sacrifice themselves for their ideal. They seek no reward – socialist endeavor is joyful and optimistic in itself – but reward crowns their efforts. Alov and Naumov's Pavel Korchagin renounces personal happiness for the sake of the new society he is helping to establish: 'this isn't the time for love', he says more than once. But the price he pays is appallingly high. Alov and Naumov cast sacrifice in highly ambiguous terms, in part by exploiting cinema's ability to convey the visual drama of illness. *Pavel Korchagin* encloses its flashback center with images of a blind, paralyzed Pavel. As the film opens, Pavel's death-mask face rests on his pillow, his skin pale, his gaze motionless. It closes with a reassuring finale, in which a healthy Pavel tells the viewer not to believe in his death. Immediately before this scene, however, the film-makers return to the prologue, showing us Pavel, blind and bed-ridden and wrestling with despair. The film underscores his losses: emotional happiness, health, ultimately life itself. Whether in *The Forty-first* or in *Pavel Korchagin*, the cost of achieving true faith appears frightfully high: one's love, one's very soul.

Historical Background

Films about the Soviet Civil War, rough equivalents of Westerns, had long been a staple of Soviet cinema. Audiences loved their verve and vigor; officials approved the clear identification of heroes and villains. By 1957, however, after the release of films such as *The Forty-first* and *Pavel Korchagin*, standard treatments seemed dated and insipid. Audiences still sought heroes on screen, but thanks to these films, to Italian neo-realism, to the 'everyday life' shown in films like *Spring on Zarechnaia Street*, they had become more sophisticated. They rebuffed the rhetorical and flamboyantly political definitions of heroism integral to the set-pieces of Soviet history; they sought heroism elsewhere. The Second World War, between 1945 and 1953 a subject almost untouched by film-makers, offered a meaningful historical context within which to elaborate heroic potential and to celebrate heroic deeds, deeds accessible to – indeed, accomplished by – millions of Soviet viewers.

As so often in Soviet culture, politics had accounted for both the earlier silence and the new energy. The Nazi invasion of the Soviet Union on 22 June 1941 devastated the country's military defenses; Stalin's reluctance to acknowledge the reality of assault resulted in horrific casualties. For artists, though, as for most of the Soviet population, the invasion removed the psychological burden imposed by the Molotov–Ribbentrop Pact: they were now free to hate Nazi Germany openly and collectively.

From 1941 to 1945, most Soviet citizens were united with one another and, at least in their perception, with their leaders: the war became the single unifying experience in a national history otherwise rent by agonizing divisions. The Nazis supplanted the bogeymen of the 1920s and 1930s – kulaks, Trotskyites and Bukharinites, assorted 'enemies of the people'. Allies who transmitted decoded Nazi secrets and shipped desperately-needed Lend-Lease supplies replaced the image of a hostile world bent on destroying the Soviet 'cradle of the revolution'. The war years summoned forth the best that people were capable of, in a common experience and for a common goal that transcended ideological and other differences, and artists played an integral role in that national effort, imbuing their work with passionate patriotism.[16]

As the Nazis pushed further into Soviet territory, in the summer and autumn of 1941, the major Russian film studios relocated to Central Asia. Together with the Georgian, Armenian and Azeri studios, they managed to produce about seventy feature films between 1942 and 1945, about two-thirds of them 'war films'. The most influential of them – Friedrich Ermler's *She Defends the Motherland* [Ona zashchishchaet rodinu, 1943], Mark Donskoi's *The Rainbow* [Raduga, 1943], Lev Arnshtam's *Zoia* (1944), Gerasimov's *The Great Land* [Bol'shaia zemlia, 1944] – featured women as their protagonists. The first three portray heroines, a simple peasant and partisans, respectively; *Zoia* was based on the death of an actual teenager, Zoia Kosmodemianskaia.[17] All of them endure horrors and torture at the hands of the enemy but remain true to their country and their cause. Gerasimov's heroine has no personal encounter with Nazis, but she becomes a first-rate worker in an evacuated factory while her husband is serving at the front because she knows that her labor contributes to victory. Each woman is, or becomes by the film's end, a canonic positive hero; as Kenez comments, 'they stand for an idealized image of Soviet womanhood and for patriotism'. These films, along with depicting the brutality of the Nazis and impressing upon audiences the need to resist, effectively defined the components of wartime cinematic female heroism: 'loyalty, constancy, endurance, self-sacrifice'.[18] *The Cranes are Flying* would respond to and challenge that definition in fundamental ways.

Once the war ended, and right up until Stalin's death eight years later, the state rewrote history. Ugly reminders of the war disappeared: police cleared the streets of crippled and begging veterans, for instance, deporting many of them to the far north. Stalin acquired retroactive stature as the sole architect of victory in ostentatious and meretricious artistic versions of the conflict underwritten by the regime. Post-war monuments and parade banners featured airbrushed images of him, as did films like *The Fall of Berlin* [Padenie Berlina, 1949]. Draconian post-war cultural policies encouraged portraits of robust, clean and bright-eyed soldiers at the front (Peter Krivonogov's 'The Victory', Ilia Lukomsky's 'The Solemn Oath of the Defenders of Stalingrad') and cheerful, confident civilians in the rear (Tatiana Iablonskaia's 'Bread', Alexander Laktionov's 'Letter from the Front').[19] Art glossed over or falsified both military mistakes and civilian miseries.

The Second World War receded from official history as the Cold War intensified. Stalin fired leading military commanders and sent others to the Gulag; he abolished Victory Day as a state holiday in 1947 (Brezhnev and Kosygin officially reinstated it in 1965). Stalin declared that the war was too recent for the necessary 'objectivity', and shut historians out of the archives to prevent challenges to the official version of events. A few writers persevered, producing a small body of honest and moving war literature: most notably, Viktor Nekrasov's *In the Trenches of Stalingrad* (1946) and Vasili Grossman's *For a Just Cause* (1952).

Until Stalin's death movies had no chance of depicting the war with integrity. In *The Return of Vasili Bortnikov* [Vozvrashchenie Vasiliia Bortnikova, 1953], the last film he made before his death, Vsevolod Pudovkin mounted an exceptional, indeed unique, challenge to conventional cinematic presentations of the war and its aftermath: his unhappy hero returns home to a wife who has given up waiting for him and has found another man. While 'industrial production' issues dominate the film, its best scenes convey Bortnikov's anguish when reality fails to meet his expectations of a new, happy life.

Then, at the Twentieth Party Congress, Khrushchev asserted that errors made by Stalin during the Second World War had cost millions of Soviet lives. A wave of memoirs by soldiers, partisans and former prisoners in Nazi camps followed, as did autobiographical fiction by writers who had fought at the front: Grigori Baklanov, Iuri Bondarev, Vasil Bykov, Ales Adamovich. Audiences and artists alike could claim a more complex and more painful history of the war, but a more accurate one as well, one that corresponded to their own experiences. In this revised history of the war, the Soviet people – not the Kremlin leadership – defeated Nazi Germany, and *all* the Soviet peoples, not just Russians, civilians in the rear as much as soldiers at the front. Khrushchev's affirmation of Stalin's responsibility for Soviet casualties empowered film-makers to depict the war trauma, previously nearly absent from the screen: *Spring on Zarechnaia Street*, for instance, shows no trace of it, even though it almost certainly orphaned many of the protagonists. Afterwards, revisionism on screen paralleled similar manifestations elsewhere. *Immortal Garrison* [Bessmertnyi garnizon], a 1956 film made by director Zakhar Agranenko with cinematographer Eduard Tisse, transferred to the screen a script by Konstantin Simonov about the defense of Brest, a city lost in the first year of the war. In *Immortal Garrison* the Soviet screen showed for perhaps the first time Russians, not only Germans, being taken prisoner; Russians, not only Germans, die in agony. The film candidly acknowledges the high price of Soviet victories and the tremendous anguish of its populace.

Film critic Iuri Khaniutin wrote forthrightly about the 'tragic errors' of the first year of the war, and about 'the stupid arrogance, the unjustified confidence in our military superiority that characterized the last months before the war'. Exploiting what proved to be a brief interval of tolerance between the Twentieth Party Congress and the Hungarian uprising, Khaniutin laid the blame squarely on the cult of personality, with its insistence that 'genius could not err', and its misrepresentations of the retreats and bungling of the first months of the war as 'careful' and 'intentional' strategy. He indicted films made during Stalin's lifetime for ignoring Soviet military failures, and for confining their definition of war to battle, thus distorting the war experience of the vast majority of Soviet citizens.[20]

Beginning with *Immortal Garrison* and climaxing (temporarily) in Andrei Tarkovsky's first feature film, *Ivan's Childhood* [Ivanovo detstvo, 1962], film-makers amply compensated for their earlier silence. They expanded the definition of conflict far beyond military engagement, and broadened their designation of war's victims to comprehend virtually all segments of Soviet society.[21]

Immortal Garrison is fairly primitive. Characters lack depth and individuality; the hero never pauses to wonder why the army has been left in such disarray. But in its portrayal of war as a nightmarish and violent intrusion into the cozy intimacy of family and friends, ruthlessly destroying 'the few remaining islands of happiness',[22] *Immortal*

Garrison moved cinema significantly closer to the major war films of 1957 and 1958, *Soldiers* [Soldaty], *The Cranes are Flying* and *The House I Live in* [Dom, v kotorom ia zhivu, 1957; see Chapter 4]. Mosfilm released *Soldiers* in January 1957. Director Alexander Ivanov stayed close to Viktor Nekrasov's script, based on *In the Trenches of Stalingrad*, with its action alternating between the battle of Stalingrad and civilians on the outskirts of besieged Leningrad. *Soldiers* has its share of clichés. Some of them come from Nekrasov's novel, although Nekrasov's dialogue is more authentic and colorful than the improbably bland curses of the screen soldiers. Others are cinematic: the silent pan of the faces of men who form the 'wall of steel and iron' that the Germans must defeat, the sweet melody of Tchaikovsky's 'Andante Cantabile', which visibly moves the soldiers.[23]

True to Nekrasov's text, Ivanov's film presents ethnicity less conventionally. Films of that period tended to subordinate ethnic to national – that is, Soviet – identity. Soviet fiction and films (*The Fall of Berlin*, for instance) featured the equivalent of the Hollywood foxhole Italian-Irish-Jewish-WASP mix, its standard assortment including a Russian (almost always the hero), a Ukrainian, a Jew, one generic Central Asian and one beak-nosed type from the Caucasus. *Soldiers* candidly acknowledges stereotypical ethnic characteristics. One soldier, who looks Jewish, is physically inept and intellectually proficient: a mathematician in civilian life, he cannot swim, ride a bike or brawl. The stereotype disintegrates when the Jew behaves as courageously as the others.

Soldiers broke precedent by openly blaming the Soviet state for the prospect of defeat. 'Ask the lieutenant commander where the Red troops are,' asks an old man in a dacha near Leningrad, his voice revealing both fear and outrage. Why, he wonders helplessly, has Leningrad been left defenseless? Egregious military and strategic blunders are committed on every level, and the corpses that line a muddy field visually spell out the result. The captain who sends his men into a daylight attack, in effect a suicide mission (and many men died in precisely such missions), is subsequently reprimanded, stripped of his authority and remanded for trial. 'You will answer for this crime,' the hero tells him, and he actually does.

For all its merits, *Soldiers* quickly forfeited its pre-eminence as a bold and original treatment of the war. *The Cranes are Flying* supplanted it. From the first screening of *Cranes* at Mosfilm in late August 1957, where it moved to tears most of the professionals in the hall, to its triumph at Cannes in 1958, where it garnered the Golden Palm Award as Best Film, *Cranes* quickly became a landmark in Soviet cinema. Arguably the best 'war film' to come out of a Soviet studio, *Cranes* transformed not simply what viewers and reviewers expected of movies that portrayed the war, but their own consideration of the war experience itself.

The Intersection of Five Careers

Cranes built on these films, to be sure. In addition, as cultural critic Lev Anninsky accurately observed, it issued from the converging creative paths of five key individuals who in one way or another embodied the metamorphoses of the thaw. The youngest, Tatiana Samoilova, daughter of stage actor Evgeni Samoilov, had not yet graduated from the Shchukin Theater School when she was selected to play Veronika. Her one previous film, *The Mexican* [Meksikanets, 1956], gave no hint of her potential, and her 'asymmetrical and rather strange' face, too 'heavy' for comedy and too 'light' for drama, hardly fit the classic canons of screen beauty.[24] Alexei Batalov, as her lover Boris, had also studied stage acting. He too came from a family prominent in the arts, and his uncle, Nikolai Batalov, had starred in several Soviet film classics (Pudovkin's *The Mother* [Mat', 1926], Room's *Bed and Sofa* [Tret'ia Meshchanskaia, 1927], Ekk's *Road to Life* [Putevka v zhizn', 1931]). By the time Batalov won the part of Boris he had already had two major screen triumphs: as Aliosha, the attractive youngest son in Iosif Kheifits's *The Big Family* [Bol'shaia sem'ia, 1954], and as the long-distance trucker hero of Kheifits's *Rumiantsev Case* [Delo Rumiantseva, 1955]. In both he seemed to typify the new thaw hero: his expressive, mobile and clever face, his lanky body, his coltish grace combined masculinity with modesty, strength with innocence.

If Samoilova and Batalov had just begun their careers, the other three had already established themselves in theater or cinema. Playwright Viktor Rozov, then in his forties, had trained as an actor before serving at the front during the Second World War, where he was badly wounded. *Cranes* is based on his first and perhaps least original play, *Alive Forever* [Vechno zhivye], written during the war. Until Stalin's death the play could be neither published nor performed because of its protagonist, 'a weak woman rather than an exemplary "positive hero" of Socialist Realism'.[25] In *Alive Forever*, as in his later plays, Rozov examined the conflict between coarse philistinism (*meshchanstvo*) and tender, childlike spirituality; the former seduces the latter, in this case Veronika, who doesn't so much betray her soldier-lover as she is betrayed by base materialists.

After the war Rozov worked as an actor and theater director, and studied at the Gorky Institute for World Literature, but his success as a playwright rested on the cultural changes the thaw encouraged. With their emphasis on humanistic and ethical values, and their young, stylishly skeptical protagonists, Rozov's dramas, and the screenplays he adapted from them, articulated some of the major preoccupations of the 1950s, and enjoyed commensurate popularity: one of his plays, *In Search of Happiness* [V poiskakh radosti], played at ninety-eight theaters in the winter of 1957–58, and set a record with 4,662 performances.

Rozov's fortunes rose and fell with the oscillations of relaxation and repression that typified the thaw years. Thus despite his earlier hits, the authorities would not permit his screenplay *A, B, C* [A, B, V, G, D, 1961] to go into production, because it depicted the culture of young people too 'negatively'. He joined the editorial board of the magazine *Youth* [Iunost'], a magazine that from its very inception, in 1955, denoted liberalism and innovation, and served until the late 1960s, when censorship had so eviscerated the journal that Rozov and other literary symbols of the thaw (Vasili Aksionov, Evgeni Yevtushenko) felt constrained to leave.[26]

But the success of *Cranes* required more than Samoilova's radiance, Batalov's decency, Rozov's dramaturgy. It needed above all the productive partnership forged by Sergei Urusevsky (1908–74) and Mikhail Kalatozov (1903–73) in the mid-1950s. Both had had separate and successful careers before they came together. Urusevsky had studied art in Leningrad (at one point with Rodchenko) before shifting into cinema as an assistant cameraman in 1935. He filmed at the front during the war, joining the Communist Party in 1942, and after the war worked with director Mark Donskoi on *Village Teacher* [Sel'skaia uchitel'nitsa, 1947]. He shot *The Return of Vasili Bortnikov* for Vsevolod

Pudovkin and *Lesson of Life* [Urok zhizni, 1955] for Iuli Raizman, both of which exhibit (albeit unevenly) Urusevsky's trademark lyrical fluidity and unpredictable montage, before giving full rein to his creativity in *The Forty-first*. Urusevsky joined Kalatozov on *First Echelon* [Pervyi èshalon, 1956] before they collaborated on *Cranes*, and their partnership continued in *Unsent Letter* [Neotpravlennoe pis'mo, 1959] and *I am Cuba* [Ia – Kuba, 1964].

Urusevsky's dynamic and lyrical camera style held obvious appeal for Kalatozov, who had relied upon comparably subjective camera and dynamic montage in his own early films, which he shot himself. Kalatozov, born Kalatozishvili, received all-round training in the film industry in the early 1920s in Georgia and in Russia. Working first as an editor and cameraman, then as scriptwriter, he debuted as co-director (with N. Gogoberidze) of *Their Kingdom* [Ikh tsarstvo, 1928], a film that used newsreel footage from 1918–20 to portray the Georgian Mensheviks who led the republic before ceding control to the Soviets.[27]

In *Salt for Svanetia* [Sol' Svanetii, 1930], Kalatozov's first major film, he used footage he shot high up in the Georgian mountains. Towering mountain ranges entirely surround a village of Upper Svanetia, whose inhabitants cannot receive the salt needed for life until the Soviet state begins to construct a road. Disorientingly acute angles cant soberly ethnographic material of villagers as they thresh barley, cut slate, hew stone, bury their dead and bear their children; extreme close-ups of the animals licking urine-splattered rocks and sweating faces for the essential salt alternate with extreme long-shots to convey the community's extraordinary isolation.

Both Kalatozov's irreproachable ideology – the greedy church that sucks the life from the village, the triumph of Soviet power ('For Bolsheviks there are no obstacles') – and features of his style (close-ups of bellies and backs ridged with muscles, dramatic montage juxtaposing the contorted facial features of a woman in labor with the superstitious rituals of a funeral) accord with the contemporary political and cinematic context developed by Kuleshov, Eisenstein, Dovzhenko and Pudovkin. *Salt* displays considerable virtuosity. Jay Leyda called *Salt for Svanetia* 'surrealist in the literal sense of the term ... with a harsh pity for the tragedies of [the] subjects that is far more moving than any appeal for sympathy'.[28] Kalatozov's images articulate his point of view: no words accompany the close-up of a breast dripping milk on to a tiny burial mound, nor are words needed.[29]

The authorities banned Kalatozov's next film, *Nail in the Boot* [Gvozd' v sapoge], for its supposed calumny of the Soviet Army. The title denotes a defective nail in a soldier's boot: the ensuing injury results in the capture and destruction of a Red Army armored train. The army court-martials the soldier, who in civilian life works in a shoe factory and may himself have been responsible for the bad boot.[30] Kalatozov defended the film for demonstrating how every aspect of Soviet life, including the army, depended on industry and workers. Nevertheless, the ban held.

The débâcle of *Nail in the Boot* and the denunciation of Kalatozov's 1936 script on Shamil – the long-time military and political leader of resistance to Russian control of the Caucasus, captured in 1859 – as a 'distortion of history' pushed him out of active film-making into various administrative posts, including a stint in Hollywood.

With the partial exception of *Valeri Chkalov* [1941], Kalatozov's creative work foundered between 1932 and 1954. (*Chkalov*, a film made with the full co-operation of the air force about a colorful pilot hero of the 1930s, displays Kalatozov's 'excitement in the "mere act of flying", plus his sympathy with a hero whose temperament often got him into trouble'.)[31] He directed *Courage* [Muzhestvo, 1939] for Lenfilm; he and Sergei Gerasimov co-directed *The Unvanquished* [Nepobedimye, 1943]. After the war he made two Cold War films, *Conspiracy of the Doomed* [Zagovor obrechennykh, 1950] and *Hostile Storm* [Vrazhdebnye vikhri, 1953; rel. 1956].

Stalin's death liberated Kalatozov. His first thaw project, *Faithful Friends* [Vernye druz'ia, 1954], with a script by Alexander Galich, was a lyrical comedy about three boyhood friends who meet up in adulthood. *Faithful Friends* broke little new ground – in that sense, indeed, it reflected the slow start that characterized the thaw within the film industry throughout 1954 and 1955. But audiences liked the film: upwards of 30 million viewers saw it in its first year.[32] It satisfied at least a small part of their hunger for films that, banal plot and schematic characters notwithstanding, portrayed their lives with some degree of veracity.

By the time Kalatozov and Urusevsky made *First Echelon*, a cross between 'frontier' adventure and love story about the Virgin Lands project, their options had broadened significantly. *Mise-en-scène* had lost much of its pomposity and artifice, and the classic good looks of the high-browed (though never highbrow) heroes of socialist realism – Martynov (Sergei Stoliarov) in *The Circus*, Chapaev's mentor Furmanov, played in the film by Boris Blinov – were yielding to the mobile features of Batalov and the cocky mischief of Nikolai Rybnikov (in, for instance, Mikhail Shveitser's *Alien Kin* [Chuzhaia rodnia, 1955]). In Kalatozov's second thaw film three young actors of varying types made their debut, and each went on to a major career: Oleg Efremov, Tatiana Doronina and Alexei Kozhevnikov.

Like all the pictures that came out in 1955 and 1956, *First Echelon* awkwardly cobbles together old and new, conventional and innovative. Kalatozov and Pogodin resisted the urge to simplify the Komsomol hero, even though screen heroes and heroines were still expected to present intact images of rectitude, to embody ideological purity. Efremov plays Uzorov as a relatively complex character, devoted to the undertaking, but also rather foolish – he seems to believe that wish and willpower alone can transform the land into productive fields. Over-confident, he magnifies the significance of slogans and directives; he lacks imagination in handling difficulties. While admirable, Uzorov lacks the iconic virtues of Soviet heroism, a deficiency noted by critics who disparagingly compared him with prototypical Soviet heroes, Maxim (the revolutionary protagonist of a film trilogy made by Kozintsev and Trauberg in the 1930s), Chapaev and Pavel Korchagin.

Kalatozov also includes one character in *First Echelon* who behaves in a cruel and boorish fashion toward a girl. None of the conventional explanations motivates his behavior: he is too young to represent the survival of pre-Soviet bourgeois values, he is not a political enemy of the state, nor pathologically sick. The film does not attribute his defects to drink, or to lack of ideological vigilance – that is, to shortcomings in the social or political realm. Rather, this purely Soviet-born and bred boy is defective in the realm of character and morality.

On the other hand, as a contemporary critic commented, Kalatozov erred in trying to satisfy the demand for 'epic scale' [*masshtabnost'*] – routinely trumpeted by the Party and its spokesmen – with mass meetings and towering infernos, however powerfully filmed. He could have skipped the artificial crowd scenes and implausible confrontations without forfeiting social significance; 'chamber drama' need not be trivial.

Moreover, *First Echelon* misrepresented the motives of those who responded to Khrushchev's call. They were not all inspired by idealism. Like the society that produced them, they did not divide up into tidy categories: nearly all irreproachably devoted, a tiny smattering 'tainted'. 'It would be wrong to suggest that the Virgin Land project and the Belomor (i.e. the White Sea–Baltic) Canal [constructed by prisoners in the early 1930s] are one and the same thing, but it would also be wrong to suggest that pure enthusiasts plowed the virgin lands.'[33] *First Echelon* should not pretend otherwise.

The ending of *First Echelon* disappointed viewers. Since the edifying role of cinema remained a paramount concern of the state, films frequently closed with an edifying speech, in which a figure of unimpeachable authority affirms to a rapt audience the achievement of a heroic feat, as if thus to validate it. Kalatozov and writer Nikolai Pogodin (a playwright who scripted *Prisoners* [Zakliuchennye, 1936], a film about the Belomor Canal project) followed this formula, the speech in this case delivered by the Party secretary, Kashtanov. A literal *deus ex machina*, he descends from the skies in the final scene to congratulate the workers for their stellar performance.

By 1956, however, both film professionals and theater audiences spurned such banalities. They had learned from Italian neo-realist movies, the final dissolves of which often suggest the continuity of life beyond the boundaries of screen or cinema. (The regime permitted liberal distribution because these movies dealt with social issues and depicted 'simple', working-class characters.) They were tired of the 'exclamation point' ending, the false resolution of Soviet films.

Like *First Echelon*, *The Cranes are Flying* blends old and new, accepted and maverick. (Stepan's final speech, for example, is hardly less problematic than Kashtanov's.) But in *The Cranes are Flying* the collaboration of Kalatozov, Urusevsky, Rozov, Batalov and Samoilova succeeded beyond all expectations. Experience seasoned innocence, energy animated maturity, visual flair created a poetry of its own to achieve a balance and harmony rarely seen on any screen, and especially Soviet screens.

Notes

1. Cited by Abraham Brumberg in 'Iconoclasm in Moscow – a Commentary', in A. Brumberg (ed.), *Russia Under Khrushchev* (New York, 1962), p. 72.
2. For contemporary analyses of the reasons for and consequences of Khrushchev's speech, see the essays therein by Richard Lowenthal, Jane Degras and Merle Fainsod.
3. Evgenii Evtushenko, 'Stantsiia Zima', *Oktiabr'* 10 (1956).
3. Harry Willetts, 'The "Literary Opposition"', in *Russia Under Khrushchev*, pp. 364–5.
4. For an examination of the reasons for the industry's minimal output, see Peter Kenez, *Cinema and Soviet Society from the Revolution to the Death of Stalin* (London, 2000) and Josephine Woll, *Real Images: Soviet Cinema and the Thaw* (London and New York, 2000).
5. See 'Iz analiticheskoi spravki ministerstva kul'tury SSSR v TsK KPSS', in T. M. Goriaeva (ed.), *Istoriia sovetskoi politicheskoi tsenzury: dokumenty i kommentarii* (Moscow, 1997), pp. 116–18.
6. Communist Party members were clearly identified as such; KGB agents were not. Val S. Golovskoy with John Rimberg, *Behind the Soviet Screen: The Motion-picture Industry in the USSR 1972–1982* (Ann Arbor, MI, 1986), p. 26.
7. 'Istochnik vdokhnoveniia', *Iskusstvo kino* 3 (1956), p. 5.
8. Lev Anninskii, *Shestidesiatniki i my* (Moscow, 1991), p. 27.
9. Ilia Erenburg, 'Uroki Stendalia', *Inostrannaia literatura* 6 (1957); English tr. in Ilya Ehrenburg, *Chekhov, Stendhal, and Other Essays* (London, 1962).
10. The worst attacks appeared in *Literaturnaia gazeta*, 22 August 1957, and *Znamia* 10 (1957).
11. Irina Shilova, *... i moe kino* (Moscow, 1992), p. 46.
12. Joshua Rubenstein, *Tangled Loyalties: The Life and Times of Ilya Ehrenburg* (New York, 1996), p. 302.
13. Maia Turovskaia, 'Marlen Khutsiev', in N. R. Mervol'f (ed.), *Molodye rezhissery sovetskogo kino: sbornik statei* (Leningrad-Moscow, 1962), pp. 179–81 passim.
14. Vitalii Troianovskii, 'Chelovek ottepeli (50-e gody)', in V. Troianovskii (ed.), *Kinematograf ottepeli* (Moscow, 1996), p. 29.
15. Ibid., p. 31.
16. See Nina Tumarkin, *The Living and the Dead: The Rise and Fall of the Cult of World War II in Russia* (New York, 1994), pp. 52–94 and John and Carol Garrard (eds), *World War 2 and the Soviet People* (London and New York, 1993). For the specific role of cinema, see I. Bol'shakov, *Sovetskoe kinoiskusstvo v gody Velikoi Otechestvennoi Voiny* (Moscow, 1950); Peter Kenez, 'Black and White: The War on Film', in Richard Stites (ed.), *Culture and Entertainment in Wartime Russia* (Bloomington, IN, 1995);

Kenez's chapter entitled 'Films of World War II', in *Cinema and Soviet Society*.
17. See Rosalinde Sartorti, 'On the Making of Heroes, Heroines and Saints', in *Culture and Entertainment in Wartime Russia*, pp. 182–91.
18. Kenez, 'Black and White', pp. 168, 169.
19. Musya Glants, 'The Images of War in Painting', in *World War 2 and the Soviet People*, pp. 110–12.
20. Iurii Khaniutin, 'Tragediia, kotoraia ne rasskazana', *Iskusstvo kino* 9 (1956), pp. 19–20.
21. The screen did not represent the special victimisation of Jews, however, until Aleksandr Askoldov's *The Commissar* [Komissar], made in 1967 but released only two decades later. For the 'history' of *The Commissar*, see V. I. Fomin, *Polka* (Moscow, 1992), pp. 46–76.
22. Khaniutin, 'Tragediia ... ', p. 24.
23. For many Russians, Tchaikovsky symbolized Russian culture. Shostakovich described the Germans' near-destruction of Tchaikovsky's home in Klin in November 1941 as an attempt by 'the Nazi barbarians ... to destroy the whole of Slavonic culture'. Cited by Boris Schwarz, *Music and Musical Life in Soviet Russia 1917–1970* (London, 1972), p. 176.
24. Anninskii, *Shestidesiatniki i my*, p. 37.
25. Wolfgang Kasack, *Dictionary of Russian Literature Since 1917*, tr. Maria Carlson and Jane T. Hedges (New York, 1988), p. 338.
26. Ibid.
27. For his early years, see German Kremlev, *Mikhail Kalatozov* (Moscow, 1964), pp. 22–57.
28. Jay Leyda, *Kino: A History of the Russian and Soviet Film* (Princeton, NJ, 1960), p. 293.
29. See Iu. Bogomolov, *Mikhail Kalatozov: Stranitsy tvorcheskoi biografii* (Moscow, 1989), pp. 42–53, for an interesting analysis of *Salt* as an example of romantic cinema.
30. No print survives; my summary is based on Kremlev, *Mikhail Kalatozov*, pp. 50–7, and Leyda, *Kino*, p. 294. (Leyda never saw the film, and bases his comments on the controversy surrounding it.)
31. Leyda, *Kino*, p. 358.
32. Sergei Zemlianukhin and Miroslava Segida, *Domashniaia sinemateka: otechestvennoe kino 1918–1996* (Moscow, 1996), p. 60.
33. V. Ognev, 'O sovremennosti', *Iskusstvo kino* 7 (1956), pp. 17–18.

3. Analysis

Characters

In this drama of a woman's betrayal, unhappiness and redemption, Soviet audiences responded first of all to the film's characters. Five of them merit particular analysis: the pair of cousins who are in their mid-twenties, engineer Boris (Batalov) and pianist Mark (Alexander Shvorin); Boris's physician-father, Fiodor Ivanovich Borozdin (Vasili Merkurev); his sister Irina (Svetlana Kharitonova), also a doctor; and Veronika (Tatiana Samoilova).

Mark

Hero Boris and anti-hero Mark conform most readily to standard types. Indeed, Mark slips into stereotype, especially in the second half of the film. He takes advantage of his uncle's trust when Fiodor Ivanovich asks him to look after the traumatized Veronika. Spurred by a jumble of fear, desire and ruthlessness, he rapes Veronika. He prostitutes his (considerable) talent and toadies to a crooked impresario. He consorts with vulgar and selfish actresses, to impress one of whom he even steals Veronika's beloved toy squirrel, her last gift from Boris. In what is revealed to be his basest action, motivated purely by fear for his own skin, he exploits his uncle's position to procure a fraudulent draft exemption.

Unquestionably Mark behaves abominably. He betrays his family, he betrays his fellow-citizens. And yet, for all his duplicity and corruption, he lacks the forceful character conventionally associated with villainy. He is weak, not wicked; he merits disdain rather than anger or hatred. Fiodor Ivanovich makes the point plainly when he dismisses Mark as a milksop for buying a bottle of port (instead of the vodka a 'real man' would drink) to toast Boris's departure. Mark genuinely cares for his cousin, although his affection does not deter his pursuit of Veronika: early on, when he meets her at the river embankment in Boris's stead, he gazes at her with longing and covers her hand with his. The Veronika of these early scenes, still happily secure in her love for Boris, spurns him confidently, almost briskly, and even makes a joke of his devotion to tweak Boris.

Until the night of the rape Mark insinuates his adoration rather than acting on it. As bombs explode and glass shatters, however, the combination of panic-stoked adrenalin and Veronika's instinctive, unsexual gesture of running into his arms emboldens Mark. He sheds his earlier passivity, tracking her down the hallway as she tries to escape, exerting his will in defiance of her slaps and repeated negatives. He overpowers her both physically and psychologically. But his uncharacteristic energy soon dissipates. Apart from his resolute announcement to the family that he and Veronika want to marry – and even then his body language, as he bends forward and addresses his uncle, suggests entreaty rather than resolution – Mark demonstrates more petulance than vigor, behaves more like a child than a man.[1]

Mark's banality, which derives from Rozov's play, troubled members of Mosfilm's artistic council when they met to discuss Rozov's script in June 1956, and again when they saw the finished film fourteen months later. In the end, they complained, Mark is no more than a run-of-the-mill deserter: the film never convinces us that he truly believes his musical talents entitle him to save himself at the expense of others, the rather extraordinary argument he uses to justify his behavior.[2]

The studio also disliked the script's linkage of artistic endeavor with corruption and cowardice: every one of the negative characters is involved in the arts. Kalatozov and Urusevsky visually emphasize that connection, filming the birthday party as a depraved carnival of physically grotesque types who seem to have strayed from a Fellini film. When actress and impresario suitor huddle in a corner for intimacy, the low source of light accentuates the actress's double

30   The Cranes are Flying

2. Mark [Shvorin] playing piano among the decadent theater crowd in evacuation.

chin; her ludicrous coquetry contrasts as markedly with Veronika's authenticity as her pudgy face and body set off Veronika's slender frame.

Indeed, by the time Veronika bursts into the party, grabs her squirrel, reads for the first time the note Boris had tucked beneath the nuts in the squirrel's basket, and smacks Mark across the face, the viewer has more or less stopped paying attention to Mark, so flat has his character become. Whereas Veronika 'continues to play her role seriously ... Mark suddenly begins to play at checkers – with every move he gives himself away more and more openly, so as to convince the viewer that he is base, craven, nasty, in no way a match for Veronika'.[3] His disappearance from the film comes as a relief.

Boris

If Mark never quite comes to life on screen, Boris transcends comparably hackneyed features, thanks in part to Batalov's acting and in part to decisions made by Kalatozov and Urusevsky on how to film him. (As everyone involved in *Cranes* testifies, they worked together so closely that such decisions must be imputed to both men.) *Cranes* exposes two aspects of Boris, one more conventional for Soviet heroes, one less. The former, resting on Boris's identification of self with nation, derives from Rozov's text, though in the play, comprising six scenes, Boris departs before the end of the second. His decision to volunteer for the army rather than wait to be drafted exemplifies this transcending of the claims of individual ego. So does his rescue of the wounded soldier Volodia, who had earlier smirked over Veronika's photograph coarsely enough to provoke Boris to punch him.

Boris's actions place him within a traditional Soviet heroic mold; as one critic wrote, he represented for viewers the generation that defeated fascism. 'Men like him reached Berlin, if they were not killed earlier, near Smolensk or Stalingrad.' Batalov, whose Boris extends but does not radically differ from his earlier characterizations in *The Big Family* and *The Rumiantsev Case*, 'expressed on screen a contemporary perception of the positive hero, a contrast to the heroes of earlier monumental cinema. He didn't try to deheroize or trivialize his hero. Batalov understood his job more profoundly. He retains his hero's nobility but imbued it with irony and a simplicity of expression. It's no accident that the young people of the 1950s felt close to his Boris.'[4]

Indeed, Boris represents a major change from Kalatozov's earlier, picture-perfect soldier-hero in the wartime *The Unvanquished*. With no creases in his clean uniform and no crack in his brave smile, that character never flinches in the face of enemy fire. Boris – exhausted unshaven face, mud-caked fatigues, slogging step – is his antipode.[5] Boris also dislikes verbal articulation of emotion, shying like a nervous horse (or – despite his twenty-five years – an adolescent) when his father calls Veronika his 'fiancée' and embarrassed by the bathos that lurks at the edge of his father's farewell toast. As in his earlier roles, Batalov's quizzical charm, eloquent face and gestures, and boyishly lanky body combine to lift Boris above cliché, to make plausible both his diffidence and his quiet but stubborn romantic idealism.

Batalov's acting perfectly captures Boris's normalcy and decency, but it never makes him other than normal. Kalatozov, despite con-

3. Boris [Batalov] embracing Veronika in the blackout scene.

ventional films like *Conspiracy of the Damned* and *Faithful Friends*, never 'relied on actors or on literary scripts. For him, film was always an adequate means of revealing his artistic concept.'[6] Kalatozov and Urusevsky complicate Boris's character through cinematic choices. First, they eliminated lines from the original script that would have vulgarized Boris. Thus they dropped a kittenish exchange about kissing ('May I?' 'No you may not,' etc.) whispered by Boris and Veronika on the staircase of her apartment house. They cut fatuous lines originally included in the death-scene fantasy, where Boris would have advised Mark that 'the most important thing is to live honestly; then even death is not so awful. Although I want to live ... '[7]

Second, they allowed image to dominate dialogue. In that scene, for example, triple exposures and swirling camera movement wordlessly evoke the future that Boris will never have, and render Boris's death – 'strange and unheroic' compared with conventional Soviet film depictions[8] – far more poignant.

Batalov himself considered Urusevsky the perfect 'thaw' cameraman, 'chosen by fate', who could use his camera to reveal the depths of human emotions and desires hidden beneath ordinary faces.⁹ Cameraman and director shared a feverish intensity quite alien to Rozov's 'water-color tenderness' (with all the implications of delicacy and attenuation that phrase suggests), a quality suggested in the film only by Batalov. Kalatozov's and Urusevsky's art adds another dimension, far more elemental and emotional, to Boris's modesty and appeal. Thus in the blackout scene, for instance, Urusevsky lights Boris and Veronika's faces to bring out a wealth of nuances that change from one shot to the next. (He used all kinds of broken glass, fingers and jars to achieve the lighting effects, Batalov recalled.) 'It's hard to count all the various faces of Veronika we see in this brief scene ... For Boris these minutes are the last he has with his beloved, and he has to see everything that he is losing.'¹⁰

Fiodor Ivanovich

Similar choices define Fiodor Ivanovich Borozdin, the character who most explicitly articulates the judgments of the film-makers. Vasili Merkurev, whom Kalatozov had worked with on *Faithful Friends*, was a veteran actor familiar to all Soviet viewers. He played in several immensely popular movies, including *The Return of Maxim* [Vozvrashchenie Maksima, 1937], Zarkhi and Kheifits's *Member of the Government* [Chlen pravitel'stva, 1940], and Alexander Stolper's *Story of a Real Man* [Povest' o nastoiashchem cheloveke, 1948]. In *Cranes* Merkurev plays Fiodor Ivanovich as warmly paternal, if sharp-tongued. Though he has only two children, Boris and Irina, he metaphorically fathers nearly every character in the film. His nephew Mark lives with him. He welcomes Veronika without hesitation after her parents' death. He sympathetically questions the two young girls who come to say goodbye to Boris and teases them with paternal good humor. After he and his family leave Moscow for the rear, where he runs a hospital, he combines his medical skills with a bracing benevolence to help wounded soldiers recover from their psychic as well as physical injuries.

In the director's script of 1956, Fiodor Ivanovich bluntly criticizes Soviet errors and mendacity in fighting the Nazis. On night duty during the war, he and a colleague stand on the roof and look up at the sky: 'The newspapers used to write that when the war started, it would be fought on foreign territory. But whose cities are burning, ours or the Germans'? We heard in all the songs, "We're peaceful people, but our armored train waits in reserve" ... What is it waiting for? Why doesn't it get moving?' His colleague Ivan Afanasevich offers the stock answer: 'The fascists invaded unexpectedly, treacherously.' 'Oh, those slippery fascists!' Fiodor Ivanovich scornfully replies, '... Oh, those nasty men! They didn't even warn us ... What, we didn't know what they were like? ... We blundered, we blundered at the beginning of the war ... we missed our chance.' Ivan Afanasevich glances anxiously around to make sure no one is within earshot, but Fiodor Ivanovich continues to yell: 'Now they print shameful reports. You can't make head or tail of them ... On the one hand, we're destroying them root and branch; on the other, we're retreating from one city after another.'[11]

Kalatozov never filmed the scene. Perhaps he feared that it was too candid for the censors. Or perhaps he eliminated it as a diversion from the core of the film: he nearly always shoots secondary characters in *Cranes* together with and in relation to Boris or Veronika.

He did include another barbed bit of dialogue from the play that fits seamlessly into the main action. When the two young girls declaim their good wishes to Boris, they speak 'in the name of the factory committee'. Fiodor Ivanovich mocks the political rhetoric that debases the genuine human feeling for which it substitutes. 'You mean to say, "Beat the Fascists, Boris,"' he says, his clenched fist beating out the rhythm of the platitudes, 'while we in the rear will fulfill and over-fulfill the factory plan!' Full of helpless love for his son, and pity for all of them, he continues more temperately, 'Never mind, girls. Better sit down and drink to my son Boria.'

Fiodor Ivanovich most clearly expresses the point of view of the film-makers in his refusal to condemn Veronika. Although her marriage to Mark obviously pains him, he accepts the news without comment: only his tightened lips betray his dismay. He never reproaches Veronika: rather, he consistently feels, and shows, understanding for her unhappiness. In the hospital, when Fiodor Ivanovich harshly censures faithless women, he is simply trying to calm a patient whose frenzy at the news of his fiancée's marriage to another man threatens his convalescence (though Fiodor Ivanovich's fervor may involuntarily reveal his own inner tensions). Veronika flees the ward, hounded by

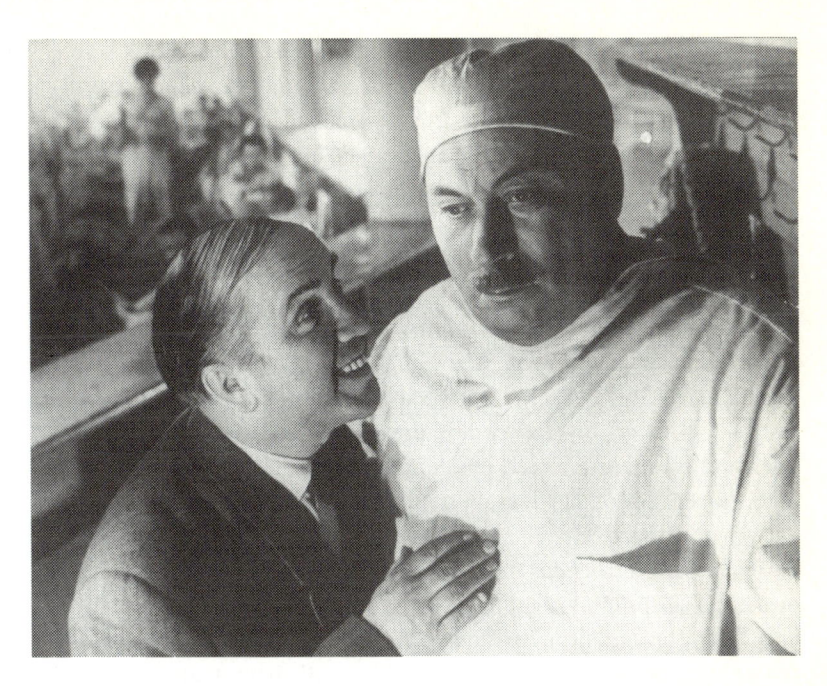

4. Fiodor Ivanovich [Merkurev] learns of Mark's perfidy from Chernov [Kokovkin].

inchoate thoughts of suicide, because she takes Fiodor Ivanovich's rebuke to be directed at her. In fact, he had no thought of Veronika when he spoke, but as soon as he looks around for her, he realizes what happened. His perception testifies to his sensitivity, just as his remorse testifies to his compassion. And when Mark's deception about the military exemption is exposed, Fiodor Ivanovich immediately assesses it as incomparably worse than Veronika's 'betrayal'; he kicks Mark out, while ensuring Veronika a permanent place in his family. In the film's final scene, Fiodor Ivanovich comforts Veronika with an embracing arm after she finally comes to terms with her loss.

Irina

Fiodor Ivanovich forgives Veronika more readily than she forgives herself, and far more readily than his daughter Irina. Irina lacks her father's charity. Having followed him into a medical career, she chose surgery as her specialty, with its emphasis on technical virtuosity over human empathy. She judges Veronika's betrayal of Boris severely, smashing a glass in disgust when Mark announces his and Veronika's imminent marriage, and she scorns what she deems Veronika's willful blindness to Mark's philandering.

During the actual war, women were the *sine qua non* of Soviet victory. All nurses and nearly half of all front-line doctors, field surgeons and medical assistants were women; in the rear, women staffed hospitals, dug anti-tank ditches, drove cranes and trucks, plowed fields, produced munitions. In and out of the armed forces, Soviet women vouchsafed their country's defeat of Nazi Germany.[12] Yet in *Cranes* Irina, despite her vocation, fails to qualify as a heroine: she is too masculine. The film presents Irina as consistently (and unnaturally) mannish, and condemns her intolerance of Veronika as a contravention of her female nature; Navailh calls them Red Virgin and Eve, respectively.[13]

The film sharpened the softer Irina of both the play and the director's script, and heightened the contrast between her and Veronika. In the evacuation barracks, for instance, when Veronika lashes out at her, calling her an 'envious old maid', Irina tearfully confides to a neighbor that it isn't true, that she had been in love with a student at the medical institute. The line was cut.

Perhaps in part because they can so easily be dramatized, gender dichotomies differentiate Veronika and Irina. Veronika tends to the injured in a feminine, nurturing capacity, while Irina's professional expertise, however praiseworthy, is explicitly characterized as manly. As she and her father, in their sex-concealing masks and gowns, wearily come out of a successful operation, Fiodor Ivanovich says, 'You should have been a man,' to which Irina replies, 'I'm all right as I am' [*mne i v devkakh khorosho*].[14] She speaks gruffly even to those she loves: she sends off her brother with a mocking salute. She lacks Veronika's maternal knack with Borka.

The visual contrast between Veronika and Irina consistently works to Veronika's advantage. Soft lighting heightens Veronika's delicacy; harsh lighting exaggerates Irina's austerity. Irina's hairstyle and military uniform desex her, while escaping tendrils of Veronika's bunned hair and her snug sweater suggest her sensuality. Indeed, Irina embodies efficiency and competence, useful qualities but far less appealing than Veronika's fragility and vulnerability.

Veronika

Until the mid-1950s, the 'film hero' unproblematically denoted the main character and his services to society and/or state. In its conventional meaning, that term cannot be applied to Veronika.[15] Veronika hardly resembles traditional Soviet female paradigms, especially those associated with war. She is far from the simple, loving and modest post-office girl Mashenka, from Iuli Raizman's 1942 eponymous film. She does not embody civic virtues, like the canonized Zoia Kosmodemianskaia, the high-school girl martyred by the Nazis. She lacks the fidelity enshrined by Konstantin Simonov in his wartime poem 'Wait for Me' [Zhdi menia], the basis of a film directed by Alexander Stolper and Boris Ivanov in 1943.[16] Simonov's 'elegiac if inelegant love poem' moved millions; 'women repeated [it] as tears streamed down their faces; men adopted [it] as their own expression of the mystical power of a woman's love'.[17]

Veronika is an enigma. Her name, unusual in Russian, derives from the Greek, 'bringer of victory', but to a Russian ear it sounds like Vera, 'faith' – yet she breaks faith. She marries one man while she never ceases to love another. We can only infer her reasons for marrying Mark: her sense of absolute abandonment in the wake of Boris's silence and her parents' death; her indifference to survival that is its consequence, most vividly highlighted in her reckless refusal to seek safety in a bomb shelter; the resignation that follows her unavailing defiance of Mark and the rape. Nevertheless, those reasons fail to satisfy, and her choice stands as the central paradox of *Cranes*, resistant to logical analysis.

Before *Cranes* such a character would have been typecast as the 'faithless fiancée', and portrayed on screen in appropriately dark hues. *Cranes* transformed a 'condemned and rejected' type into the subject of 'astonishing sympathy and admiration'.[18] The war makes Veronika a victim, it causes Boris's death, yet it cannot destroy her love for him. Thus a film about betrayal becomes, paradoxically, a film about fidelity, a film that assigns 'absolute supremacy' to feeling. In his note, Boris – the man who evaded high-flown language, who wryly excluded jealousy ('I have no time for it') – clearly states his love for her. His love appears to be stronger than his death: love seems to transcend reality itself.[19]

As the Russian film scholar Evgeni Margolit observes, Veronika signifies the intrusion of nature into the social world. *Cranes* – like most Soviet films – defines every other character socially, either by familial role (the granny) or by profession (doctor, actress, factory worker, soldier). Veronika, however, is not student or worker or nurse, though she talks of becoming an architect, takes a job in a factory, helps in the hospital during evacuation.[20]

Even less conventionally, particularly within the cinematic tradition of wartime heroines, the larger meaning and repercussions of the war leave Veronika indifferent. She cares only about its effect on her, so loth to lose Boris that she encourages him to try for an exemption on the basis of his cleverness or his professional status. She has no social ideal – one reason why Irina dislikes her – nor is she an intellectual: abstract ideas do not interest her at all.

Veronika has no identity except as an incarnation of love. She loves her parents, she loves Boris, she loves the child she rescues, Borka. She instinctively mistrusts the corrupt impresario with whom Mark allies himself in evacuation. Like the cranes, who operate on genetically coded drives, Veronika is an animal creature, propelled by instincts and impelled by feelings. And like another immensely popular contemporary film character, Zbigniew Cybulski's Maciek in Andrzej Wajda's *Ashes and Diamonds* [Popiół i diament, Poland 1958], both Veronika's salvation and her despair lie not in what others know, but in her own subjective faith. In the Soviet cinema of those years, where individual emotions 'easily accommodated themselves to the collective', Veronika's trust in her own feelings virtually made her unique.[21]

A system of stereotypes regulated and balanced the cinematic realism of the 1950s, populated mainly by well-managed paradigms re-educated in the spirit of socialist ideals. Thanks to Veronika, *Cranes* breached that system, but not without controversy: debate swirled around her, admiration for her vying with angry denunciations of the 'faithless woman' as heroine. Either way, the film's refusal to pass judgment on Veronika compelled viewers to form their own judgment of her, and by extension of themselves. She became a new yardstick, particularly for viewers her own age.

For Neia Zorkaia, doyenne of Soviet film scholarship, *Cranes* told 'the story not of a glorious exploit but of guilt and atonement. The central character of the film could under no circumstances ... be a

5. Veronika [Samoilova] imagining her wedding.

"positive example", yet the authors refused to pass judgment on the girl Veronika who, under tragic circumstances, betrayed the memory of her bridegroom killed at the front.'²² Samoilova herself interpreted Veronika as 'a pure person whom it was wrong to hurt or offend ... who was deprived of all her innocence by one catastrophe after another ... who died a little bit every day of the war'.²³ Certainly the Veronika Samoilova played on screen bears little resemblance to the Veronika of Rozov's play, a pallid and uninteresting young woman.

And just as Batalov injected his own particular personality into the familiar contours of Boris, so Samoilova – with her unusual beauty, the 'lightness and grace of her full figure', the apparent spontaneity of her acting ('she seemed to *be*, not to act')²⁴ – made of Veronika a woman quite distinct and individual,²⁵ the thematic and stylistic center of the movie. 'If Rozov's spiritual tenderness revealed itself in Batalov,' Anninsky wrote, 'and Urusevsky embodied on screen Kalatozov's (and his own) feverish passion, then Samoilova combined these two sources, their paradoxical clash.'²⁶ In the opinion of Maia Turovskaia, Samoilova herself, with her canted eyes, her gravity, the 'childlike simplicity' of her face – rather than unhappy, stubbornly loyal Veronika – became the embodiment of Russian young womanhood for the entire world.[27] 'In the final analysis', as Irina Shilova wrote, the film dealt not so much with betrayal, nor with how others judged Veronika, but with 'the right to live one's own life – perhaps unhappy, plundered, ravaged, but one's own. It had been an unacceptable idea for entire generations, which had embraced the demands of common, communal, civic obligation.'[28]

Style

Samoilova did not create Veronika by herself, although her distinct individuality suited Kalatozov. 'When you leave the theater,' Turovskaia commented, 'you don't know whether the image of Veronika owes her charm to ... Samoilova's talent and sincerity or to Urusevsky's art, able to catch in the turn of a head, a momentary pose, the blink of eyelashes, the helplessness and obstinacy, the tenderness and pride of this particular woman's character.'[29] Like all great cameramen, Urusevsky scrutinized faces as if they were landscapes, tracing the contours of Samoilova's countenance with the same painstaking care he devoted to the desert in *The Forty-first*, and would later devote to the Siberian taiga in *Unsent Letter*. When his camera concentrates on Veronika it regains the freedom the directors of the 1920s exploited, with fragmented images, extremely short takes and rapid montage.

Indeed, the visual drama of *Cranes* stunned audiences as much as its choice of heroine disconcerted them. Urusevsky and Kalatozov brought back to Soviet screens a kind of film-making that had been absent for nearly thirty years, the exceptionally dynamic and vibrant romantic cinematic language that had characterized some of the best Soviet cinema in its first decade. 'The usual organization of a frame disappeared, as did customary, easy to decipher *mise-en-scène*, composition, lighting. Everything shifted from what had seemed to be their only possible places. The screen became alive, animated, unmediated.'[30]

Once again, responsibility devolves on both Kalatozov and

Analysis 41

6. Veronika's last happy smile as she opens her birthday present.

Urusevsky, with their common understanding of movement as the essence of cinema. (Movement, as Semion Freilikh observed, can take many forms: dynamic montage, chiaroscuro, the expressiveness of the human figure shot from extreme angles; neither Kalatozov nor Urusevsky was afraid to deform or distort material to produce a certain effect.)[31]

Kalatozov's early training behind the camera made him particularly receptive to Urusevsky's genius; both men instinctively sought cinematic means of expression, rather than dramaturgic, narrative or even thespian. As a result, changes from the play to the director's script and from the director's script to the completed film consistently tone down the overly explicit and eliminate blatant statements. Kalatozov dropped a dialogue between two interior voices in Veronika's head as she runs to the station, for instance: one signals her overwhelming guilt ('You're vile [*podlaia*], guilty') and her wish for death ('not to suffer any more'), the other affirms her wish to live ('you are not guilty ... death means impotence [*bessilie*]').

Together he and Urusevsky manipulated lighting, camera and montage in ways that the script does not even indicate, such as dissolving from Mark's feet crunching through the glass to Boris's boots slogging through the mud. Batalov recalled that when Kalatozov and Urusevsky planned the joyful opening scene, they wanted to pan across a pre-dawn sky that would fill the entire screen. The day they filmed the sky was overcast, conveying a different mood. Kalatozov and Urusevsky omitted the shot, rather than compromise its effect.[32]

Salt for Svanetia had no thematic common ground with *Cranes* – its hero is the group, not the individual. Yet Kalatozov employed many cinematic elements that we see in *Cranes* thirty years later. Kalatozov begins *Salt* with an abstract and undefined 'always' – life in the high Caucasus has always been like this. Time suddenly intervenes with an explicit date: 28 July 1929, 'a hot day'. *Cranes*, too, begins in a timeless present. In reality Muscovites, like all Soviet citizens, no matter how 'normal' their lives in the spring of 1941, worried about the possibility of war, yet no intimation of war mars the opening sequence of *Cranes*. As a result the public declaration the next day shocks us as much as it shocks the Borozdin family. Mark's agitated announcement as he tried to shake his cousin awake ('Boris! Boria! It's war!') foreshadows the destruction of innocence, even though Boris himself remains unaware, shrugging Mark away with a sleepy 'So what?' [*nu i pust'*].

In *Salt*, a film virtually devoid of plot, Kalatozov varied high- and low-angle shots, extreme long-shots and extreme close-ups, in order to create drama, a pattern that characterizes *Cranes* as well. Kalatozov's visuality marked even his least interesting movies: in the 1939 *Courage*, an implausible spy thriller that showcases few of Kalatozov's gifts, he cut together a sequence of sky and landscape shots in an accelerating tempo to create a sense of rising excitement, much as several shots of a woman combing the fleece of a sheep in *Salt* suggest the rhythm of her work – and as the montage of feet, fence, smoke and snow contributes to the rising tension of Veronika's suicide run.

Urusevsky did not always film so fluidly. For director Iuli Raizman he shot *Cavalier of the Golden Star* [*Kavaler zolotoi zvezdy*, 1951], a classic of late Stalinism with 'no conflict except a contrived romantic one, no drama except the forced drama of electrification, and almost no action'.³³ But the broadening of thematic opportunity that formed so integral a part of the thaw emancipated Urusevsky's camera. (His work in *The Return of Vasili Bortnikov*, Vsevolod Pudovkin's swansong of 1953, intimates what was to come.) A list of his pre-*Cranes* work – *Village Teacher, Cavalier, Bortnikov, Lesson of Life* [Urok zhizni, 1955], *First Echelon, The Forty-first* – reveals 'how the Man with the Movie Camera "thawed", how his vision individualized itself'.³⁴

Evgeni Margolit observed that as long as heroes embodied inert amalgamations of primarily civic virtues, cinematography remained static and frozen. Once movies could explore 'the inner human condition, that is, the *movement* of the human spirit [ital. EM] ... cinematography regained its earlier dynamism'.³⁵ Beginning with *The Forty-first* and *First Echelon*, Urusevsky's camera became supple and flexible. In all of Urusevsky's later work, both the two films that he and Kalatozov made together after *Cranes*, *Unsent Letter* and *I am Cuba*, and those he directed himself (*The Trotter's Race* [Beg inokhodtsa, 1968] and *Sing a Song, Poet* [Poi pesniu, poèt, 1971], he filmed rural landscape, city streets and human faces as not merely countryside, urbanscape and physiognomy, but as windows into or mirrors of human psychology.

The long takes and pans that Urusevsky preferred produce uninterrupted images, 'an unusual illusion of presence ... the depth and layering of space,' and effectively eliminate from our awareness the limits of the screen,³⁶ the way Caravaggio's figures break out of conventional framing to enter our space. Thus after the bombing of her building we run up the stairs alongside Veronika, look with her eyes through the bombed-out ruin to the cityscape outside, see the dangling lampshade, understand with her that her parents have been killed. The camera becomes her shadow, her double, and resonates with her emotions. Since it continually returns to the same locations (Krymsky Bridge, the staircase in Veronika's building), it penetrates her inner world as much as it records the outer one.

Nowhere does Urusevsky create this effect more tellingly than when Veronika rides the bus to say goodbye to Boris. As she sits on the bus, looks out of the window, frets at the delay, jumps off, the camera remains close by, no more than a step or two away from her. Suddenly – though without editing – the camera cranes up, gazing down at the street to show us a tiny figure – black hair, light dress

44 The Cranes are Flying

7. High-angled crane shot of Veronika and the anti-tank defenses ('porcupines').

– slipping between the enormous rumbling tanks. Normally this would indicate a shift from interior point of view to an external, authorial point of view. Somehow, in this scene, that shift does not occur. Instead we remain both with Veronika and watching her, as the 'bottomless funnel of the war – made out of iron, dust and smoke – begins to engulf her and suck her in'.[37]

Much earlier, when Veronika walks away from Mark on the embankment, Urusevsky shoots from high above the riverside: a small girl in a black sweater, threading her way through the X-shaped defenses ('porcupines'). 'The war hasn't yet done its work, Boris is still at home, but a paralyzing premonition of loss, of separation and betrayal, can already be sensed, a slowly spreading invisible stain.'[38]

Urusevsky's nervous, dynamic (often hand-held) camera, the flow of frames that creates a sense of constant motion, and the rapid changes of point of view matched Kalatozov's romantic sensibility, his plasticity. The cinematographer described the process as 'thinking in images', intended to bring the viewer into the tension of the scene. When Veronika runs away from the hospital, the canted frame 'enhances the unnerving effect and the tension produced by the medium shots of Veronika running away toward the train station that alternate with close-ups of her feet stamping the snow'.[39] The images jar and lurch against one another in a disorienting mix of blurred shapes. Urusevsky explained:

> The suicidal person doesn't pay attention to people on the street. He is in a condition of nervous shock, a condition that every person has experienced, though not necessarily in its most extreme form. In other words, the person's inner state expresses itself in how he perceives the world. Why not show this on screen? Here 'abstraction' becomes a means of conveying an entirely concrete human experience.[40]

In the *provody* (departure) sequence, one of *Cranes*' most famous, camera movements combine panning, tracking and high-angle crane shots, 'systematically shifting point of view from external (the eye of the camera) to internal (Veronika's and Boris's)'.[41] The camera glides along the horizontal plane of the fence, climbs it along with Boris, presses up against it with Veronika, making it – like the Odessa pier in *Battleship Potemkin* – unnaturally, almost infinitely long, contrasting its rigid verticals with the 'uneven, rustling human mass'.[42]

Almost no dialogue intrudes. Twice Boris is told that Veronika will turn up ('*da pridet ona*'), a wife tells her husband to 'write, write every day', we hear a couple of shouts and snatches of phrases, the question, 'Who has the requisition for the cauliflower?' Finally the commands: 'Attention!' imposes order, 'Forward march!' begins the transformation of this mass of civilians – husbands, fathers, brothers, sons, lovers – into soldiers, their now synchronized steps belying the diversity of their dress, their headgear, their possessions. But if dialogue nearly vanishes, sound does not. For the first and only time in the film, sound contributes as much to the meaning and power of the sequence as do camerawork and editing.

Sound

Elsewhere in *Cranes*, Kalatozov consistently subordinates sound, both diegetic and non-diegetic, to image. Non-diegetic sound occurs only a handful of times, usually as musical background in emotionally charged scenes. The film begins with non-diegetic sound: Boris and Veronika hop along the newly-washed squares of Moscow to a brightly cheerful and optimistic tune. When Veronika leaves the bomb shelter and races through the ruins and up the skeletal stairs to her parents' flat, ominous chords crash. The thunderous Rachmaninov with which Mark tried to drown out the explosions continues after he jumps up from the piano, melodramatic obbligato to the repetition of slaps and negatives Veronika hurls at Mark before he snatches her up in his arms and she falls back limply. Strings accompany the whirling birches and wedding celebration of Boris's death-fantasy, and a pounding agitated score, articulation of Veronika's disordered thoughts, attends her run toward the trains.

In all these cases Moisei Vainberg's music has no source within the film. It serves conventional 'background' purposes, suits itself more or less hyperbolically to the actions and emotions depicted on screen. But in the *provody* dialogue, Kalatozov layers diegetic music with words in an aural articulation that matches the camera as it dollies down the crowd and cuts between Veronika and Boris. At first we hear a few bars of 'Katiusha', the pre-war tune that enjoyed immense popularity among Soviet citizens and abroad as well: Italian partisans fighting against the German occupiers adopted it for themselves.[43] 'Katiusha' fades into other snatches of songs, including a traditional *chastushka* sung only by women, along with the handful of lines mentioned above; each sound-segment is briefly audible, just as the camera records each face as it passes, without lingering. Eventually the sounds become indistinguishable from one another, and then the band begins to play the 'historically charged and habitually heartbreaking "Farewell of a Slavic Woman" [Proshchanie slavianki]. Noise of this sort – carrying no information *per se* ... produces an unnerving effect,'[44] as do frequent shots of Boris, vainly scanning the crowd for Veronika and then, defeated, looking down at the ground. A woman's voice (not Veronika's) calls out 'Boria! Boris!' but the name registers on his hearing no more than Veronika's soundless cry of his name. 'He neither sees nor hears her, as if literally belonging to a different spatial [and aural – JW] dimension already – the war space as opposed to the home front.'[45] Like a full stop ending a paragraph, the cookies Veronika throws toward Boris fall unnoticed to the ground, crushed by marching feet. Her inability to give him her gift fits into *Cranes*' sequence of missed opportunities: his failure to present her with the squirrel himself, her failure to read his note until much later. As the screen fades to black, sound becomes silence.

Structure

Rozov's play, *Eternally Alive*, consists of six scenes, the first two and the last set in Moscow, the middle three in evacuation. All six occur in indoor spaces, Veronika's and the Borozdins' apartments in Moscow or the barracks, and Rozov heavily relies on symmetry as his principle of dramatic structure. The Borozdins' selflessness and dedication diametrically oppose the materialism and egoism of Chernov and Monastyrskaia, the actress; Veronika and Irina, with about the same number of lines, are roughly equal in importance. Boris appears in the first two scenes, thematically contested by Mark, but a replacement for Boris occupies the last two scenes: Volodia, the wounded soldier who in the play is Anna Mikhailovna's son. Rozov's Volodia does not come purposely to tell the Borozdins of Boris's death but rather to see his mother; he simply mentions the soldier who saved his life, and how he spoke of the woman he loved, whose nickname was 'Squirrel'.

Predictably, Kalatozov opened up the film by including half a dozen scenes in public spaces. He retained symmetry as a narrative and to an extent as a visual principle, but discarded much of the secondary plot involving the actress Monastyrskaia. The film is shaped like an hourglass, with Boris's death the center or fulcrum of the film, its second half an inverted reflection of the first.[46]

1. Dawn

Boris and Veronika wander the empty streets of Moscow, near the river; Boris points to a flock of cranes flying overhead, and Veronika recites her poem before kissing him lightly. They skip along, carefree as children. A street-cleaning truck sprays them with water; Boris wrings out Veronika's soaking hair. He drapes his jacket over her shoulders and they walk away from the camera.

In this opening sequence private emotions harmonize with public spaces. The two lovers need no one else (though their relationship hardly seems sexually charged) yet they are part of the Moscow landscape, inscribed into it by the composition that places them along the embankment, in the square, alongside the church. Nothing clouds their happiness. The credits roll against a bright sky while Kremlin bells chime six.

2. Homecoming

The camera stays very close to Boris and Veronika as they enter Veronika's building, whispering partly so as to avoid disturbing the inhabitants and partly because Boris's love is expressed in restrained gesture and gaze, an early indication of his distaste for 'fancy' words. Veronika, though younger, controls the situation, keeping him silent with a finger to her lips, making a date for later that week by using her fingers. The space is neither public nor private, but something between.

Veronika enters her home on tiptoe, the camera nipping at her ankles and following her down a cluttered corridor. As she steals past her parents, her mother disapprovingly whispers, 'He's turned her head,' to which her sleepy husband replies, 'And she his. That's love.' In her room, adorned with a photo of poet Vladimir Mayakovsky, Veronika stretches exuberantly and falls flat on to her bed.

Boris, in his home, nibbles food from a pot on the stove. The apartment is still quiet, but his grandmother has begun her daily routine, Irina is awake enough to comment snidely about his nighttime activities, and Mark – with whom he shares a room – wants to know if Boris has torn his jacket. Boris, exactly mirroring Veronika, stretches before falling into bed, happy.

With its fold-out sofa and the communal hallway, Veronika's home is more typically Soviet than the Borozdins', who occupy the comfortable flat of a family of Moscow *intelligenty*. But warmth, domesticity and family intimacy fill both interior spaces. Boris and Veronika are loved, and safe, at home. The sequence ends, however, with the intrusion of public life into that safe domestic sphere: as the Borozdins (minus the still sleeping Boris) sit around the table, sipping tea and chatting amicably, they hear the war announcement, and Mark tries to wake his cousin.

3. Embankment; trench

A pair of outdoor scenes follows. The first reveals to us Mark's hopeless passion for Veronika, and her resolute rejection of him (to a crescendo of romantic piano music); she walks away between the anti-tank barriers, menacing X-shaped iron constructions. In the second, Boris digs trenches alongside his factory-mates. Stepan, his best friend, tells him 'the notice' has not yet come, and asks if he has yet told Veronika. (We don't yet know to what he refers.)

Both scenes touch on the matter of exemption from military service. Mark says exemptions will be given to those deemed 'more valuable' and that normal life must continue; Boris tells his colleague that the latter's experience and knowledge will win him an exemption, while his mate responds that Boris's talent makes him more deserving.

These two scenes contrast Mark and Boris visually as well as thematically. Mark wears a sports jacket and clean shirt; Boris is sweaty and dirty. Mark lolls back on the parapet; Boris stands upright or bends over his spade. Neither here nor anywhere else in the film, with the exception of the birthday party, is Mark seen with any friends, while Boris works amid a group of men, laughs with his co-worker, confides in Stepan.

4. Blackout

The private space of Veronika's bedroom is enhanced by the blanket Boris and Veronika hang over the window. Yet paradoxically, in these moments of greatest intimacy, each is masking anxiety from the other. Boris hides the fact that he has volunteered; Veronika conceals her fears for him with an 'insistent gaiety', a childlike and almost play-acting frivolity.[47] As they tease each other and dream about the future, we see a myriad of expressions on Veronika's face, from playful to triumphant, from tender to confident, as if in these last minutes they have together 'Boris must see everything that he is losing'. As soon as Stepan discloses the truth, Veronika's face closes up, and though Boris tries to caress it back to its former expressive mobility, he cannot. The barrier later symbolized by the fence already separates them.[48] Reiterating the morning scene, neither wants to let go of the other; they can't say goodbye, he can't turn and leave, yet they do not manage to tell each other their most important thoughts.

5. Toast

A private scene, engendered and shadowed by public circumstances. Boris's departure is the scene's *raison d'être*, and everyone pitches in

8. Boris, Veronika and Stepan [Zubkov] in the final moments before Stepan reveals that they've volunteered.

to prepare him: Irina irons his shirts, Mark wraps his scarf around his cousin's throat. Boris occupies center stage when he writes Veronika a birthday message at his desk (presided over by a small bust of Lenin) and conceals it under the gold nuts in the toy squirrel's basket; he entrusts Granny with the gift, as well as with looking after Veronika should she need help. (We never discover what happens to Granny.)

But Boris, who awaits his father's return with some trepidation, becomes almost peripheral as soon as Fiodor Ivanovich comes in, his emblematic paternity enhanced by Urusevsky's careful camerawork.[49] In the director's script, as in the play, Fiodor Ivanovich received a phone call at the hospital telling him to hurry home, but the scene was dropped, presumably as superfluous. Instead Dr Borozdin strides into his apartment, obviously agitated. He brusquely chides his son for rushing headlong into war ('Twenty-five years old, to be such a fool?!'); he needles him about Veronika. Neither exasperation nor anger masks his profound love and anxiety for his son. Urusevsky moves his camera around the apartment to include one or more of the other characters throughout the scene, but keeps Fiodor Ivanovich as the visual axis of almost every shot.

Each time the doorbell rings Boris expects Veronika, and is chagrined when first Mark comes in (with his bottle of port) and then the two factory girls, bringing bundles for Boris and the Komsomol rhetoric of staunch optimism that Fiodor Ivanovich burlesques. Just after Boris removes the photo of a radiant, smiling Veronika from his desk drawer to take with him, Kalatozov cuts to Veronika herself, on the bus and then in the street, her body straining to traverse these public spaces to reach Boris. She fails. Boris marches off to the departure point amid laughter and fanfare, accompanied by Mark, Irina and the factory girls; Granny calls his name 'one last time'. Fiodor Ivanovich – symbol of every parent sending a son off to war – slumps at the table, alone in his desolation, framed by the doorway of the now empty apartment, before returning to the hospital. And

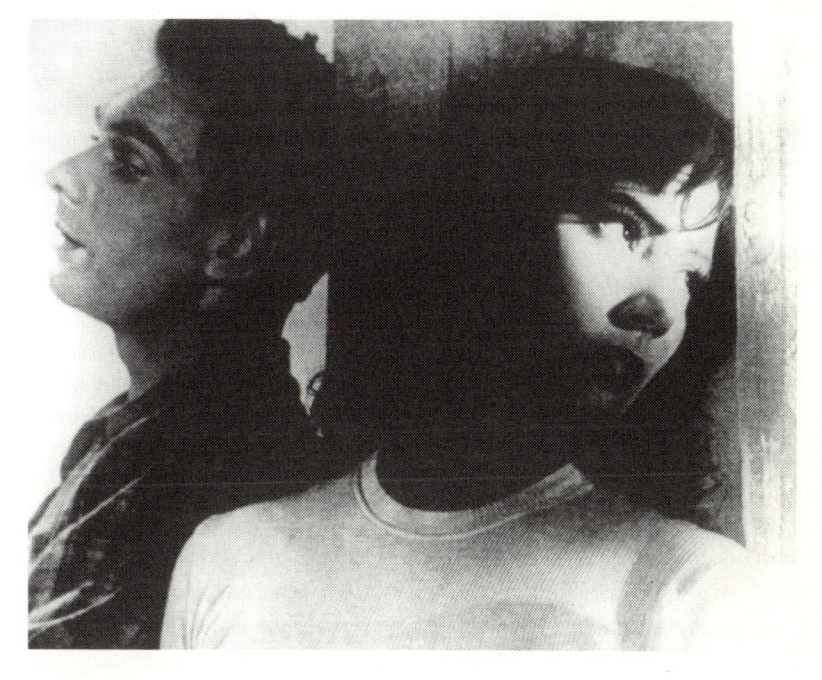

9. Boris and Veronika, separated by their private anxieties.

10. Irina [Kharitonova], the factory girl and Boris as he leaves the Borozdin apartment.

when Veronika finally arrives, so intent on her goal that she barely sees Granny, she spins on her heels and rushes headlong off to find Boris, clutching the squirrel in one hand and the cookies she bought for him in the other.

6. The *provody*

Part of this sequence's power derives from the simultaneity of public domain and private emotions. Kalatozov and Urusevsky give each absolute legitimacy; neither yields pride of place to the other until the very end, when public inevitably dominates. Urusevsky pans a heterogeneous crowd, dollies at close-up range down a horizontal line that includes newlyweds, sedately middle-aged couples, young parents with toddlers, aged parents of grown children. The fence separates only Boris and Veronika, not the others who have come to say goodbye, yet these two, 'who can't reach each other either visually or aurally, are bound together more intimately than ever before, more than they could have been during their placid young happiness'.[50]

The ferocious desire that propels Veronika through the jam-packed crowd contrasts with her frozen stance when she realizes she will not reach Boris. Urusevsky transfixes her face and hands, pressed nearly through the bars of the fence, like a deer paralyzed in a car's headlights. Her despairing cry of 'Boria!' unheard, she remains within her private universe, while Boris willy-nilly joins the column of marching men.

7. Four short scenes
The first and last form a frame of parallels. In both, Veronika (wearing a dark coat; we will not see her in light clothing until the final scene) stands in a phone booth. The first time, she inquires of Granny if there's been any news from Boris, since she's had no word. She and her waiting mother walk home between two lines of 'porcupines' [*iozhi*], x-shaped metal and barbed-wire anti-tank obstructions.

As an air raid alert sounds, Veronika's parents send her to safety in the metro station while they remain in their flat so Veronika's father can finish some work. While the camera pans the frightened citizens huddling in the bomb shelter, and Veronika makes plans to get a job at Boris's factory, a direct hit destroys her apartment building, and kills her parents.

Thus the public invades and destroys the safety of their home, and the security of their love, for each other and for their daughter. Veronika, confronting the Daliesque void that once housed her life, covers her ears against the ticking clock (an instance of symbolic sound that did not appear in the director's script), but she can neither reverse time nor blot out its damnable meaning. From this nightmare she cannot awake.

After the Borozdins take her in, and Fiodor Ivanovich confides her to Mark's special care, Veronika phones Boris's factory, with results as fruitless as when she called earlier. This time, Mark waits for her outside the phone booth, and they both walk away between the barriers.

8. The rape
In a sense the rape sequence, preceded by the bombs that shatter the windows, reproduces the devastating intrusion of public into private that occurred in the previous sequence, ratcheting up the emotional

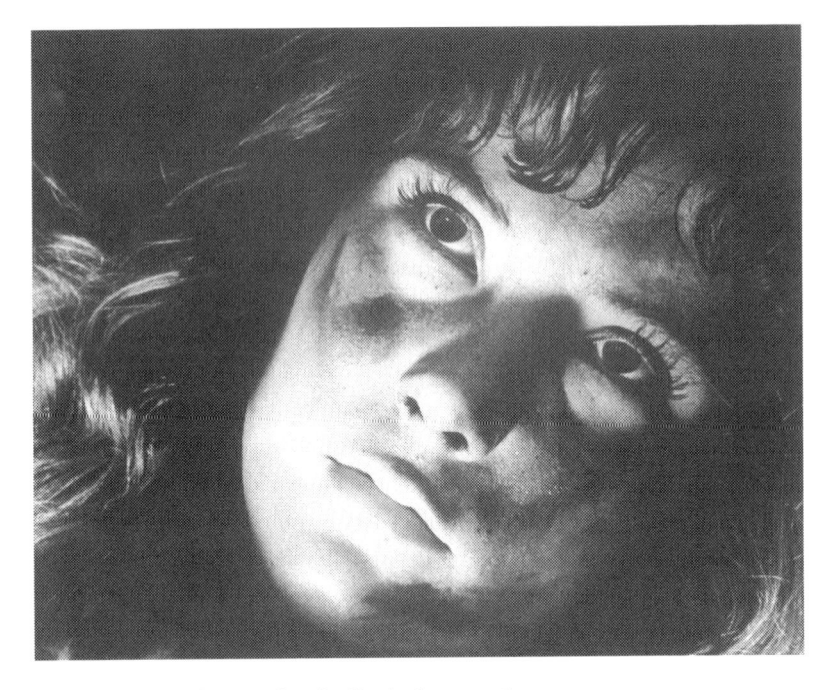

11. Veronika after the family flat is destroyed.

intensity several notches. For Anninsky this 'absurd' and 'melodramatic' scene remains effective nevertheless, not as the portrait of a woman's 'fall', but as the 'tragedy of war, crashing down on the most defenseless, naïve soul'.[51]

Maia Turovskaia, on the other hand, considers the rape scene as false as the *provody* scene is true: 'The entire aesthetic of this scene, with its melodramatic sound and light effects, with the slaps and Mark's grotesque obstinacy ... comes from some other, invented war.'[52] (Little of the overwrought melodrama, such as the slaps, the string of negatives, and the crunching glass under Mark's feet, appears in the director's script.) Nor does the rape justify or even fully explain Veronika's marriage, which Mark announces to the Borozdins just before we see Boris die.

Certainly Mark's 'dark passion' metaphorically suggests the cruelty of the war, against which Veronika's desperate resistance is futile. 'Veronika says "No" to Mark, to the war, to fate, to grief, to suffering, to everything that already exists. Visually, despite specks and brief shafts of light, blackness triumphs. The bursts of light also constitute a "No" to what exists.'[53]

The cut from Mark's feet to Boris's boots creates a symbolic continuity of space in what is otherwise discontinuous and it magnifies 'the betrayal motif'.

> That the film obscures the fact of rape is due not only to the general taboo on sexual violence in Soviet films of the time [but also because] it is not the fact of rape that seems crucial but rather its public perception as a betrayal. Given that Mark is Boris's rival over Veronika, the air raid scene foregrounds a double betrayal: Mark's explicit betrayal of his cousin away at war, and Veronika's implicit betrayal of her fiancé.[54]

9. Boris's death

Kalatozov sets up what Anninsky calls this 'great requiem' with a rather contrived dust-up between Boris and Volodia, the latter a wisecracking newcomer to the unit. Once again Boris appears amid friends (he is helping carry a stretcher), and his commanding officer, though he 'punishes' Boris and Volodia by sending them out together on a reconnaisance mission, obviously respects him. After entrusting his photograph of Veronika to Stepan, Boris sets out, eventually carrying on his back the wounded Volodia, whom he teasingly reassures ('We'll dance at your wedding').

It is, instead, his own wedding he sees in his mind's eye. As Boris's back arches from the impact of the sniper bullet, the birch trees begin to swirl. Urusevsky keeps his camera tilted up, shooting the trees against the sky from a low angle that reflects Boris's own physical stance, but also his perception of them as romantically elongated.[55] He runs up the stairs of Veronika's house in his filthy fatigues, as he ran up them in the early-morning scene. With Volodia's cries for help as a *basso continuo* underneath the strings, the apartment door opens to reveal Boris in the frock coat and Veronika in the dress and veil of her blackout imaginings, and they float down the stairs together in a delirious blur of blissful faces, raised glasses, luminous light.[56]

After Boris's death, and despite our consistent – indeed, increased – sympathy for Veronika, the film loses much of its dramatic power. The first half of the film consisted of moments of piercing happiness

12. Boris's death.

or tormenting anguish. In the second half life becomes 'physically perceptible duration: a series of steps, actions, days. It becomes a process of waiting.'[57] Cinematic poetry yields to theatricality, and the inversion of earlier scenes occasionally seems formulaic. Thus, for example, the earlier panning shot of women when Veronika takes shelter from the air raid recurs when Urusevsky pans the evacuees gathered at the train station in Siberia – again we are given to understand how war victimized vulnerable civilians. Urusevsky's camera remains free and flexible only when it is trained on Veronika; otherwise it becomes more rigid as the dramaturgy becomes more conventional.

A few scenes merit particular attention, however, among them Veronika's truncated conversation with the history teacher Anna Mikhailovna. The front room of the barracks where the Borozdins are quartered is a relatively public area, shared with many other evacuees, but the loft offers enough privacy for Veronika to express her despair to Anna Mikhailovna. Here Kalatozov dropped a line from Rozov's play that alters profoundly the impact of the scene, if not of the entire film. In the play, a deeply depressed Veronika queried Anna Mikhailovna about the 'meaning of life', and received the following answer: 'Perhaps its meaning consists in what remains after us. Go to work, Veronika, don't look for answers inside yourself, you won't find them there. And you won't find justification either.'[58]

Kalatozov did not drop the question, posed by a foregrounded Veronika. And Anna Mikhailovna begins to reply: 'Perhaps its meaning ... ' But at that moment Mark bursts in, and the question remains unanswered. Thus the film omits the pat response provided by Anna Mikhailovna, her insistence on the primacy of the social over the personal. Indeed, by implication *Cranes* contradicts that answer: it suggests that no single answer exists, that Veronika must seek and find an answer for herself and within herself. In the Soviet Union of 1957, political as well as aesthetic tradition still pressured artists to articulate clear and ideologically sound judgments. *Cranes* refused to comply, raising many questions, but providing few clear-cut answers – thus departing from Rozov's far more conventional play.

After Mark's entrance and their disagreement about Chernov, which ends in Veronika wishing aloud that Mark had never been born, Chernov himself enters. In the play he spies the squirrel and makes the suggestion that Mark take it along as a present for Antonina; in the film, he's no less venal (he asks Mark to obtain drugs from Fiodor Ivanovich) but Mark himself filches the toy: Chernov merely suggests that Mark find some small gift (*pustiachok*) to add to the box of candy he provides.

In the clean if overcrowded hospital, Veronika takes dictation from one man, gives another a bedpan, turns up the radio for a third – in other words, she provides a caring feminine presence, not medical skill. Close-ups of Veronika's face alternate with middle- and long-shots of the wounded men, all united in support of Fiodor Ivanovich's stentorian lecture to the hysterical soldier about worthless, faithless women. The doctor play-acts the gruff martinet to stiffen his patient's resolve: he follows his ringing declarations with a soft-voiced instruction to provide the now calm soldier with fresh tea. If he is also partly sincere, he certainly has no specific thought of his own son in his mind, and Veronika's flight genuinely dismays him.

The suicide-run functions as an answer to and expiation of

Veronika's failure during the *provody*. Again she runs, but where she lost Boris, she now saves Borka, as well as herself. When she asks the child his name a train whistle obscures his first reply, making her reaction when she hears 'Borka' that much more dramatic. The humor of their exchange breaks the tension: when Veronika asks 'Whose boy are you?', Borka answers 'Mama's'; to a question about his age, he replies that he is 'three months and three years' old. In the director's script he is given lots of brothers (Vanka, Vaska, Fedka etc.), but the final version distracts far less from the emotional poignancy of the scene. (Kalatozov retained an absurd list of names, but transferred it to the patient who dictates a letter home, where it fits far better.) Borka's spontaneity continues when, back in the barracks, he spurns Irina's clumsy attempts to pacify him.

Saving Borka marks the first stage in Veronika's turn away from passivity toward life. Though her own pain makes her lash out at Irina (just as a heart-broken Kitty Shcherbatskaia, in Tolstoy's *Anna Karenina*, deeply wounds her sister Dolly out of her own depression), she decisively rejects Anna Mikhailovna's suggestion that she wait for Mark to clarify the matter of the squirrel: 'I'm tired of waiting, I've been waiting all my life.'

The restoration of the squirrel, and Boris's note, finally kiss awake the groggy princess. As single-minded in her pursuit now as when she entered the Borozdins' apartment the day Boris left, she snatches Boris's note to her out of the desecrating pudgy hands of Antonina's guest. After the first words Batalov's voice takes over from hers, and she hears him express his love for her, a love unaffected by her betrayal. His words give her a gift beyond forgiveness, beyond death. Fully liberated at last, Veronika defies Mark's pleas for decorum, and atones for her ineffectual slaps during the rape scene with a few resounding, full-blooded whacks. (Her expiation satisfies even Irina, implicitly: when she packs to move out, Irina tries to restrain her.)

Veronika's maturity, the courage she has finally found, expresses itself in her decisive gestures as she yanks laundry off a line no less than in her willingness to rent a room for herself and Borka. She has grown up, and she tells Fiodor Ivanovich so: she no longer wants to live under the shelter of someone's wing (*za chuzhoi spinoi*). Her decision to stay becomes precisely that, a decision, rather than an action taken for lack of an alternative.

With Volodia's arrival the war re-enters the home, this time as testimony to Boris's death. The chores that occupy Veronika – laundry, Borka – belong to domestic space, and both her words and gestures seem natural and appropriate. Kalatozov (and/or Rozov) did not find the equivalent for Volodia: his words are clumsy, his actions – particularly pulling out his harmonica – off-key, as if Kalatozov wants to make sure we remember who he is. And since Volodia had actually smirked over Veronika's photo, we are entitled to wonder why he does not recognize her.[59]

The script version of *Cranes* ended with an unwieldy sub-plot: Borka's mother returns for him, and Fiodor Ivanovich reassures the disconsolate Veronika that her care for Borka was right and good, even if in the end she has lost him. She and Volodia meet Mark on the street, and – following the play – Mark accuses Volodia of being the reason Boris was killed.

Instead of these distractions Kalatozov preferred a clear inversion of the *provody*: jubilant soldiers returning, joyful crowds massing, Veronika once more jostling her way through. (The location – the train tracks – also echoes her attempted suicide.) During the *provody*, however, Veronika physically contradicted the crowd's movements, and literally thrust herself against the crowd, oblivious to everyone and everything except Boris. This time, despite her personal sorrow, she unites with the throng, smiling through her tears. Finally persuaded – by the photo in Stepan's pocket – that Boris is dead, she hands out her flowers to soldier and civilian alike, those who fought their way to victory and returned, those who survived their war in the rear, and waited. A low-angle shot of the cranes flying overhead completes the circle of symbol and feeling ushered in by the wedge of flying birds at the start of the film. Whether or not Veronika responds to Volodia's obvious love for her, she is – as Fiodor Ivanovich's consoling embrace makes plain – no longer alone.

While Stepan delivers his speech relatively informally, and with real feeling, as if addressing family or friends rather than co-workers or Komsomol members, the speech itself belongs to the already fading cinematic formula of rhetorical set-pieces. Endings routinely posed problems for Soviet film-makers, for a mixture of political, ideological and aesthetic reasons. The Ministry of Culture continually reiterated cinema's educational mission, and edifying valedictory addresses provided an easy – if banal – solution. Semion Freilikh sardonically described the worst excesses of the tradition, as manifested in late-Stalinist films:

> [Such] endings illustrate the victory of the fallen hero: he rises again to raise the banner in battle, or races along in a tank, or, as is often the case in historical/biographical films, stands embronzed on a pedestal while grateful scions (usually Pioneers) lay flowers at the base. If the hero survives to the end, he then assumes a monumental stance, directing his gaze into the future, thus illustrating his communion with the life of the next generation.[60]

For Maia Turovskaia, the finale completes the film formally, but fails to resolve it. 'What is it?' she asked. 'The apotheosis of the heroine? But she does not deserve apotheosis. Perhaps she is leaving behind spiritual isolation – but isn't it too late for that? ... If the filmmakers want to say that despite grief, a strong spirit can find within itself riches to give people, one would have liked to see that developed in the course of the film and not just as a final fillip.'[61]

Given *Cranes*' pattern of fall and rise, of death and resurrection, however, its ending is inevitable (as well as more delicate than Turovskaia allows). With its romantic sensibility, its tendency towards extremes, each fall becomes a plunge, from the relatively trivial wounding of Volodia and hysterics of the soldier to Borka's nearly being run over and the overheated violence of Veronika's rape. And each fall requires a suitably dramatic rise – Volodia's rescue, the patient's calming, Veronika's snatching up of the child. Thus Veronika's salvation must match the magnitude of her betrayal and the guilt that drives her toward suicide. (Her moral fall-and-rebirth resembles that of Tolstoy's Natasha Rostova in *War and Peace*, just as her suicide attempt reminds us of Anna Karenina's).[62] Rescuing Borka from the truck begins the process; reading Boris's loving, forgiving note continues it; distributing her bouquet completes it. 'The heroine's reconciliation with life, and its with her, must not simply occur; it must be *sanctified*. Something must occur in the nature of the spiritual ascension of a soul rescued from non-existence.'[63] Something does.

Notes

1. In her generally excellent essay Françoise Navailh offers a provocative – though to my mind unpersuasive – reading of Mark as 'the stereotype of the evil Jew', an 'alien body', and of the film as anti-Semitic. '*Quand passent les cigognes*: Histoire d'un malentendu', *De Russie et Ailleurs* (Paris, 1995), pp. 65–7.
2. RGALI Fond 2453, op. 3, delo 619, 17 June 1956, and delo 620, 27 August 1957.
3. German Kremlev, *Mikhail Kalatozov* (Moscow, 1964), p. 182.
4. Semen Freilikh, 'Proshloe i budushchee', in L. N. Poznanskaia (ed.), *Letiat zhuravli* (Moscow, 1972), p. 8. In a considerably more vulgar but fundamentally similar interpretation, Mikhail Kuznetsov comments that Boris, even in the war scenes, confounds the notion that man is merely 'a slave of circumstance, as the naturalists would have it; amid the bitterness and gloom of the war strides the Soviet soldier ... ' *Geroi nashikh fil'mov* (Moscow, 1965), p. 59.
5. Kremlev, *Mikhail Kalatozov*, p. 174.
6. Lev Anninskii, 'Akter v "rezhisserskom" fil'me', in E. Zakharov (ed.), *Akter v kino* (Moscow, 1976), p. 149.
7. RGALI Fond 2453, op. 3, delo 617: 68. This text is the 'director's script', which indicates camera placement, editing instructions etc., as well as dialogue.
8. Freilikh, 'Proshloe ... ', p. 6.
9. Alexei Batalov, *Sud'ba i remeslo* (Moscow, 1984), p. 133.
10. Vitalii Troianovskii, 'Chelovek ottepeli (50-e gody)', *Kinematograf ottepeli* (Moscow, 1996), p. 50.
11. RGALI Fond 2453, op. 3, delo 617: 41–3. When Mosfilm discussed the script on 17 June 1956, this scene was not mentioned; presumably it had already been cut. See RGALI Fond 2453, op. 3, delo 619.
12. See essays by John Erickson and Katherine Hodgson in John and Carol Garrard (eds), *World War 2 and the Soviet People* (London and New York, 1993).
13. Navailh, '*Quand passent ...* ', p. 63. Julian Graffy disagrees, finding Irina more sympathetic, an 'interesting and basically positive alternative version of the female experience of those years. Because she is not so attractive she has to sublimate all her energies into work and self-sacrifice, common enough for Soviet women of the time and something they could also respond to. Her principled refusal to forgive Veronika for abandoning her brother for her ne'er-do-well cousin is no harsher than Veronika is to herself.' Letter of 25 September 2000.
14. Graffy interprets Fiodor Ivanovich's comments as referring to Irina's unrefined language rather than her surgical skill: she says that her patient would be guilty of swinishness [*svinstvo*] should he die after all her

efforts during the operation. And he thinks that her discarding of surgical mask and robe reveals her femininity.
15. Troianovskii, 'Chelovek ... ', p. 50.
16. At a conference of dramatists and film directors held in June 1942, a ministry bureaucrat summarized a proposal for a filmscript – presumably Rozov's, though the author is not identified – almost identical to *Cranes*. 'The theme takes a wrong turn, the emotional experiences are false, and what is more, the entire ideological concept is wrong ... [Whereas in *Wait for Me*] the theme of fidelity is treated with lyricism and authenticity ... That is why we rejected the project of the former film and commissioned Simonov to write a screenplay based on *Wait for Me*.' 'The Cranes that Did not Fly in 1942', *Kinoglaz* 1 (1993), p. 30.
17. Richard Stites, *Russian Popular Culture: Entertainment and Society Since 1900* (Cambridge, 1992), p. 101.
18. Irina Shilova, 'Pobeda i porazhenie', *Kinovedcheskie zapiski* 17 (1993), p. 48.
19. Troianovskii, 'Chelovek ... ', p. 52.
20. Evgenii Margolit, 'Peizazh s geroem', in Vitalii Troianovskii (ed.), *Kinematograf ottepeli* (Moscow, 1996), pp. 106–8.
21. Troianovskii, 'Chelovek ... ', p. 56.
22. Neya Zorkaya, *The Illustrated History of Soviet Cinema* (New York, 1991), p. 212.
23. Tat'iana Samoilova, 'Èto, bylo moe ... ', *Kinovedcheskie zapiski* 17 (1993), p. 40.
24. Freilikh, 'Proshloe ... ', p. 7.
25. Irina Izvolova felt that a more conventional actress might have created a character whose grief would blur indistinguishably into the general grief of the nation. 'Drugoe prostranstvo', in *Kinematograf ottepeli*, p. 80.
26. Anninskii, 'Akter v "rezhisserskom" fil'me', p. 153.
27. Maia Turovskaia, 'Tat'iana Samoilova', in *Aktery sovetskogo kino* (Moscow, 1966), p. 213.
28. Shilova, 'Pobeda i porazhenie', pp. 48–9.
29. Maia Turovskaia, '"Da" i "net"', *Iskusstvo kino* 12 (1957), p. 14.
30. Maia Merkel', *V sto sorok solnts* (Moscow, 1968), pp. 8–9.
31. Freilikh, 'Proshloe ... ', p. 6.
32. Batalov, *Sud'ba i remeslo*, pp. 121–2.
33. Stites, *Russian Popular Culture*, p. 120.
34. Iurii Bogomolov, *Mikhail Kalatozov: Stranitsy tvorcheskoi biografii* (Moscow, 1989), p. 158.
35. Margolit, 'Peizazh ... ', p. 106.
36. Maia Merkel', *Ugol zreniia* (Moscow, 1980), pp. 27–8.
37. Troianovskii, 'Chelovek ... ', p. 48.

38. Ibid., p. 46. Maxim Shrayer, in his study of the graphic triangular compositions that characterize *Cranes*, comments that when Veronika walks into the triangle formed by the porcupines, 'she is literally drawn into the triangular space of betrayal, which also represents the home front, surrounded by the space of war'. 'Why are the Cranes Still Flying?', *Russian Review* 56 (July 1997), p. 433.
39. Shrayer, 'Why are ... ', pp. 435–6.
40. Sergei Urusevskii, 'Prostranstvo èkrana', interview with A. Lipkov (*Sovetskii èkran* 1968), reprinted in *Iskusstvo kino* 3 (1980), p. 113.
41. Shrayer, 'Why are ... ', p. 432.
42. Batalov, *Sud'ba i remeslo*, p. 134.
43. Stites, *Russian Popular Culture*, p. 104.
44. Shrayer, 'Why are ... ', p. 432.
45. Ibid.
46. Lev Anninskii, *Shestidesiatniki i my* (Moscow, 1991), p. 41.
47. Kremlev, *Mikhail Kalatozov*, pp. 166–7.
48. Troianovskii, 'Chelovek ... ', pp. 42–3.
49. Kremlev attributes the success of this scene, and the father's depiction, entirely to theatrical means, primarily acting, and not at all to cinematography (*Mikhail Kalatozov*, p. 196). Obviously, I disagree.
50. Troianovskii, 'Chelovek ... ', p. 43.
51. Anninskii, 'Akter v "rezhisserskom" fil'me', p. 153.
52. Turovskaia, '"Da" i "net"', pp. 15–17 passim.
53. Kremlev, *Mikhail Kalatozov*, p. 178.
54. Shrayer, 'Why are ... ', p. 434. For a sociological interpretation of the rape, see Brett Cooke, 'Acquaintance Rape in Kalatozov's *The Cranes are Flying*', in Simon Karlinsky, James L. Rice and Barry P. Scherr (eds), *O Rus! Studia litteraria slavica in honorem Hugh McLean* (Berkeley, CA, 1995), pp. 69–80.
55. Evgenii Andrikanis, 'Kinematograf poèticheskoi obraznosti', *Iskusstvo kino* 3 (1980), p. 90.
56. For Troianovskii, 'Chelovek ... ', pp. 46–7, the editing in Boris's death scene contradicts the rest of the film, which respects the boundaries of 'real space' and the unity of action even when it enters characters' minds, such as Veronika's entrance into her bombed flat. Urusevsky normally achieves viewer identification with a character by allowing a shot to last for so long that 'you suddenly gulp from the unexpected sensation of transcendent closeness to another soul, naked and glimmering'.
57. Bogomolov, *Mikhail Kalatozov*, p. 179.
58. Victor Rozov, 'Vechno zhivye', in *V dobryi chas: p'esy* (Moscow, 1973), p. 553 (Scene III).
59. Graffy speculates that Volodia may be a debased and then redeemed

double of Mark. The montage links them repeatedly, cutting from Mark's piano playing and the rape to Volodia, practicing on his harmonica and from Mark's announcement of the marriage to Volodia, piggyback on Boris. In effect, both bear responsibility for his death, although only Volodia asks forgiveness as Boris dies.

60. Freilikh was comparing such endings unfavorably with the ending of Chukhrai's *The Forty-first*. 'Pravo na tragediiu', *Iskusstvo kino* 12 (1956), p. 25.
61. Turovskaia, 'Tat'iana ... ', p. 18.
62. See Navailh, *'Quand passent ... '*, p. 62.
63. Bogomolov, *Mikhail Kalatozov*, pp. 172–3.

4. Reception

Cranes belonged to an evolving cinematic process in the Soviet Union, as well as to the more general cultural metamorphoses of the late 1950s. It stood out from its peers, as much because of its breathtaking visuality as because of its unusual failure to explain, justify or condemn the heroine's betrayal of her beloved. At the same time it epitomized the romanticism of the early thaw years, which flourished in films like *The Forty-first* and *Pavel Korchagin*. It actively influenced film-makers, especially younger cinematographers, and it contributed to the development of 'poetic' Russian cinema in the early 1960s and to the efflorescence of poetic cinema in the Soviet republics a little later. Critics continued to debate the manner, if not the fact, of its artistry; officials continued to cite its ideology – as interpeted by them – approvingly.

With a foray into historical documents, plus a dollop of imagination, we can place the film within its historical and cultural context of 1957–58. We can see it with approximately the vision of Soviet critics and the Soviet public, before it attained the status of a 'classic', with all the uses and abuses such status engenders. The effort is worthwhile, since it helps us both to understand contemporary reactions to *Cranes* and to assess its role in Soviet cinema.

Colleagues and Competitors

Seasoned film professionals saw *Cranes* first, a few months before its general release. Kalatozov screened the film at Mosfilm on 27 August

1957, to an audience of directors, writers and editors. They went wild. Sergei Iutkevich chaired the discussion that followed, and the minutes record nearly unanimous plaudits. (Virtually the only criticism pertained to the banality of Mark's character.) 'We all wept,' director Grigori Roshal said, 'I too wept, and I'm not ashamed to admit it.' Mikhail Romm concurred: despite the movie's 'profound optimism', he said, he wept throughout the screening. At a loss for words – though hardly speechless – these men, individually and collectively, offered tributes to Kalatozov, to Urusevsky, to the actors, to everyone concerned. 'It's not just a good [*khoroshaia*] picture, it's not just an excellent [*velikolepnaia*] picture, it's an astonishing [*porazitel'naia*] picture,' one participant commented with restraint.¹ For him, and for the others present, *Cranes* seemed single-handedly to redeem the panegyrics and pastiches, the compromises and fumbles of Soviet cinema.

Cranes opened officially in October, and *Iskusstvo kino* greeted its release with a group of articles, most though not all laudatory. Rostislav Iurenev, a generally conservative film historian who became a bulwark of the State Institute of Cinematography, contrasted the authenticity of *Cranes* with earlier war films, often monumental in scope, that exaggerated Stalin's role and ignored or minimized the exploits of individual soldiers. Certain critics had disparaged what they called *Cranes*' 'formalist flourishes'; Iurenev deprecated those critics, in turn, as people reluctant 'to speak to artists in their own language, people accustomed to clichés'. Instead, he ardently defended Urusevsky's unconventional camerawork and the film's *mise-en-scène* (the 'inauthentically' – so critics charged – empty streets): 'All these unusual aspects are part of a form developed precisely in order to convey the delicate, ineffable spiritual states of the heroes, for which words are inadequate. It is the language of cinema.'² He reserved virtually his sole objection for the fence in the *provody* scene: to him it suggested a separation between the front (the soldiers) and the rear (the civilians), whereas in actuality the war had joined those at the front and those in the rear 'in a common fate'.

A few commentators resisted the appeal of *Cranes*, typically on ideological grounds. Director Alexander Zarkhi is best known for his collaboration with Iosif Kheifits on *Baltic Deputy* [*Deputat Baltiki*, 1937] and *Member of the Government* [*Chlen pravitel'stva*, 1940], although he continued to make well-received films into the 1960s: *Heights* [*Vysota*, 1957], *My Younger Brother* [*Moi mladshii brat*, 1962]. Zarkhi exemplifies a man shaped by Bolshevik ideology and firmly wedged into Stalinist cultural politics. However much lip-service Zarkhi paid to the revelations and reforms of the Twentieth Party Congress, he could not surrender familiar categories and concepts: the politically idealistic positive hero who can and will change society, the privileging of script over camera, the opposition of a 'shallow' [*melkii*], 'hermetic' [*zamknutyi*], and 'petty bourgeois' [*meshchanskii*] world-view on the one hand, to 'scale' [*masshtabnost'*] and commitment to the larger world [*bol'shoi mir*] on the other.

In Zarkhi's view, *Cranes* reinforces the ongoing trivialization of the heroic image on the Soviet screen. When a hero like Chapaev or Shchors perishes, the viewer's eyes fill with tears: 'But these are not tears of passive sympathy. Not at all! [Whereas] many of our recent films play on the viewer's feelings with what is no more than a fancy collection of sentimental tricks ... And this superficial poignancy redounds to the praise of the film-maker ... ' In the best Soviet films, Zarkhi believes, the heroes' personal lives reflect the life of their society, and the film-makers express a militant, revolutionary stance. Regrettably, newer Soviet films consider their themes from a disquietingly passive point of view – including the 'talented' and 'interesting' *Cranes*. Kalatozov makes us sympathize with his appealing, suffering heroine. 'But no matter how hard the film-makers try', Zarkhi laments, Veronika lacks 'the special quality to be found in the new individual ... she lacks the spirit of our times'.[3]

Other critics, albeit a minority, shared Zarkhi's objections. But not all of *Cranes*' critics had retrograde agendas. As mentioned in the previous chapter, Maia Turovskaia, a consistent champion of individual cinematic vision, objected to the jarring effects that marred *Cranes*, most particularly the rape scene. Turovskaia argued that by gradually shrinking *Cranes*' emotional scale, Kalatozov had diminished the power of the film. Fidelity ordinarily concerns only those immediately involved. But it surrenders its private dimension and takes on a broader significance during wartime, because in war's exigent circumstances 'a woman's loyalty expresses the victory of the human spirit over forces of destruction and death'. The more exclusive Veronika's despair, the more inconsequential it becomes.[4]

Shortly after Mosfilm released *Cranes*, the Gorky Studio brought out a rival to *Cranes*, *The House I Live in*. The theme of *House* – in essence, the war's impact on non-combatants – overlapped with *Cranes*, leading to inevitable comparisons. *House* is a far more conventional movie, both thematically and cinematically. As a result, viewers often preferred it to *Cranes*. Its very familiarity and realism reassured those who found the iconoclasm of *Cranes* disconcerting, not entirely successfully executed, or not entirely agreeable.

Iosif Olshansky won the 1956 All-Union Competition for the best scenario with his script of *The House I Live in*, his first to be produced. Gorky Studio assigned the job to Iakov Segel and Lev Kulidzhanov, a team of relatively young men (both then in their early thirties) who had earlier co-directed a moderately successful drama, *That's How It Began* [Èto nachinalos' tak, 1956], about a group of Moscow Komsomol members who volunteer for the Virgin Lands project in Kazakhstan.

House divides its story into pre-war life, portrayed as a generally happy period, and wartime, which abruptly and violently disrupts that life and destroys that happiness. The 'house' of the title, a pristine new building when the film opens in 1935, brings together a cross-section of the Soviet population, and functions as a metaphor for Soviet society in general. A worker, his wife, daughter Katia and young son Seriozha move in first as the film begins; a bourgeois family comes next, the philistine mother disdainfully branding Seriozha a hooligan because he greets her spick-and-span daughter with a well-aimed spitball. Next door to the workers are representatives of the artistic world – Ksenia Nikolaevna, a celebrated older actress – and the technical intelligentsia – a geologist and his wife. (*House* projects back into the 1930s the adventurous geologist, a favorite heroic figure of film and fiction throughout the late 1950s and well into the 1960s – as late as Kira Muratova's 1967 *Brief Encounters* [Korotkie vstrechi]) Neighbors help one another, offering nails and spare furniture to newcomers, forming at least a social network and at best real friendships.

By and large, pre-war life proceeds smoothly and amicably in the film; no shadow of the purges, for instance, falls on the sunny passage of years. The trucker who helped the workers move in and flirted with their daughter Katia becomes her suitor and then her husband;

small children get bigger, as marks on the doorjamb indicate. Seriozha, the worker's son, continues to tease Galia, the bourgeois daughter, eventually – predictably – falling in love with her. As one critic approvingly commented, the details convey the spirit of an era: 'How good our Soviet life is.'[5]

Not that even the good Soviet life flows entirely unimpeded. Dmitri, the geologist, and his wife Lida love each other, but their dreams and their values differ sharply. Dmitri's frequent and lengthy field-trips frustrate Lida, and she belittles his commitment to his work – of which she knows so little that all rocks look the same to her. She has deferred having children to give them time alone as a couple, a choice the film decisively condemns. As against her egotism, Dmitri articulates (and acts on) a selfless, service-oriented philosophy of life: 'After all,' Lida says, 'we only live once.' 'Yes,' he responds meaningfully, 'only once. That's the whole point.'

During one of Dmitri's absences, a deeply unhappy Lida sleeps with Seriozha's older brother Kostia, an army officer home on leave, a lapse she bitterly regrets. The neighbors all know what's happened. Kostia and Seriozha's mother ostentatiously fails to greet Lida the next morning in the kitchen and remains cool toward her, literally for years; Seriozha angrily dismisses Kostia's justification that he loves Lida. But his father judges less harshly, saying compassionately, 'You can't dictate to the heart,' and teenaged Galia does not judge at all: she admits she does not know what she would do in Lida's place. The film censures Lida less for her infidelity, because it arises from her profound dissatisfaction, than for her childlessness, a result of her self-absorption.

Adultery may transpire in normal life, even in the Soviet Union. War does not. *House* introduces the war melodramatically, with flaming digits (1941) that rise up to fill the back of the screen. Crowds mass at a bus stop to listen to Molotov's radio announcement of the Nazi invasion, broadcast nationwide over loudspeakers, and the intimacy and individual focus of the first part of *House* yield to the public canvas. The *mise-en-scène* shifts from the apartment house, with its chamber dramas, on to the street; the camera steps back, abandoning close-ups and middle-shots for long-shots.[6] (The cinematographer, Viacheslav Shumsky, had worked with Segel and Kulidzhanov on *That's How It Began*.)

By placing familiar characters in new, public contexts – Lida and Dmitri among other silent couples, Seriozha in a long line of soldiers on skis – the camera suggests the totality of the war effort. Galia's parents, along with many residents, leave during the general evacuation of Moscow, but Galia refuses to abandon her city and sneaks back to her empty, icy apartment. Seriozha, home on a two-day pass, finds her sleeping there, wrapped in everything she owns and half-starved because, staying in Moscow illicitly, she has no ration card.

Iuri Biriukov's stirring score, partly instrumental and partly vocal, with the voices of the mighty Red Army Chorus in the background, enhances the quasi-documentary aspect of the war scenes in *House*. So does one of the most famous Soviet wartime images, a recruiting poster of a woman's face emblazoned with the words, 'The motherland summons!' All segments of the population respond, eagerly and in unison: fighting-age men, the shadow of whose heads cross the poster in an endless line; under-age kids who try to enlist; civilians who practice defensive maneuvers and dismantle fences for fuel.

In the film's wartime, as happened during the actual war, public and private merge in a rare harmony. Almost immediately after moving in to the apartment the worker had hung on the wall wedding pictures of himself and his wife. Now, as he leaves for war six or seven years later, the camera lingers on those pictures, motivating his readiness to serve. He will fight for the sake and future of his family, not to fulfill political and social obligations. The logic is inescapable and emotionally compelling: in order to save his beloved wife and the 'house' they live in, he must leave her, and it.

House presents victory, when it finally comes, in similar fashion, via one soldier simply coming home to his wife and child. Public spectacle takes a literal back seat as fireworks blaze in the sky beyond the window: the camera's focus is Katia's trucker-husband, stretched out on the sofa, 'too tired to take [his] clothes off',[7] while Katia runs off to fetch their daughter Maika, just an infant when her father left for war. Tears of joy fill Katia's eyes as she returns to find her husband fast asleep, and whispers to the child she holds in her arms, 'That's your daddy.'

The war leaves many gaps in the house, in the society the house symbolizes. The worker husband/father perishes; so does Galia. Seriozha's brother Kostia receives a serious wound. Dmitri is reported missing in action, and never returns. The terrible losses of the war notwithstanding, the film merges generations to create a sense of continuity, and to sustain the image of a coherent, united nation. In its epilogue, set in 1950, Dmitri's example has inspired Seriozha to become an equally dedicated geologist. Lida, after ten years of guilt and expiation for her act of betrayal, finally accepts the possibility of a new life with the steadfast Kostia. Kostia's mother acknowledges Lida's moral rehabilitation: 'He loves you, you know,' the older woman says, tacitly pardoning Lida and granting her permission to get on with her life.

In one of the last pre-war scenes Seriozha tells Dmitri about his literature exam:

> We had three themes: the image of Pechorin [from Lermontov's *Hero of Our Time*], the 'new man' from Chernyshevsky's *What is to be Done*, and one other. Not from books, our own. Your favorite hero. I decided to write about you. Because for me a hero is a person who ... well, let's say who doesn't wait to be called but sets off on his own, and where he goes factories may go up, or a whole city, but he's ahead of everyone else, he goes first, he looks for iron, bauxite, oil. Not for himself, but for other people. I didn't write it, of course. There it's all about Pechorins and Onegins. They'd never understand.[8]

Dmitri, sitting in the foreground of the frame, hardly hears him, preoccupied as he is by the note in which Lida informs him that her unhappiness has driven her to leave him. (She gets as far as the railway station before changing her mind, and they both pretend the note never existed.) Thus on the one hand *House* contrasts a boy's romantic notions about heroism with the excruciatingly complicated emotional reality of adulthood; on the other, the film uses that complexity to enrich rather than simply to reject Seriozha's definition.

House achieves much of its power from its directness. Kostia's return from the front, for instance, laconically conveys the difficulties of post-war adjustment: he stands framed in the doorway of the apartment, while the camera cuts to a steeply angled shot of his crutch clattering down the stairs. The film implicitly evokes and rebuts Laktionov's meretricious painting 'Letter from the Front', where a cheerful crowd smilingly gathers to hear the news. In *House*, women meet the mail girl with a far more authentic tense anticipation; two receive letters, while the third moves away in stoic disappointment. A scene when Galia, an aspiring actress, recites a speech to her elderly mentor, Ksenia Nikolaevna, nicely contrasts false romanticism and real heroism. Galia's voice, gestures and facial expressions are theatrical and overstated. Ksenia Nikolaevna 'corrects' her by responding (with a speech from Chekhov's *The Seagull*) so naturally that Galia mistakes the actress for the character she is playing. Art, the film intimates, should not be artful, but lifelike. Galia absorbs what Ksenia Nikolaevna teaches her: when she leaves for the front, she says goodbye to Ksenia Nikolaevna quite simply, ready for 'the ordinary Soviet girl's' heroism without fanfare or histrionics.[9]

At the Gorky Studio's discussion of *The House I Live in*, in October 1957, Kulidzhanov, Segel and Olshansky received kudos for revealing the nobility often overlooked in 'unremarkable' individuals, and for depicting the patriotism and integrity of the characters, 'ordinary' people living in 'ordinary' houses.'[10] Unlike Kalatozov and his Veronika, they had created protagonists who fit comfortably within the Soviet framework that proclaimed every individual a candidate for heroism.

Stanislav Rostotsky, one of the younger generation of directors with one 'kolkhoz' film under his belt (*Land and People* [Zemlia i liudi], 1955), contrasted the accessibility of *House* to the cunning embellishments of *Cranes*. In *House*, he commented appreciatively, a 'generalized symbol of great emotional force grows out of extraordinarily simple things that are clear to every ordinary person, who doesn't care about aesthetic questions'. *Cranes* is rather more 'Western', he added, by which he meant no compliment.[11]

Like-minded colleagues praised *House* for presenting 'for the first time' the war as it actually affected people's lives, and for its authentically 'socialist realist style'. 'In my opinion,' one man observed, 'our studio comes out ahead in this competition.'[12] *House* epitomizes art that enables the viewer to 'forget that it's art', unlike the self-conscious *Cranes*: 'Everything [in *Cranes*] is done with verve [*likho sdelano*],' one participant said, 'but one can clearly see that it's "done!" Instead of thinking about the contents of the film, you strain your memory and make every effort to remember what piece comes from where!' He exempted from his general disapproval only two supposedly 'artless' scenes, the *provody* and Veronika's return to her bombed-out apartment. In his view, Urusevsky shot these scenes at conventional angles, without 'craft' (in the sense of 'artifice': *bez lukavstva*), which accounts for their emotional impact.[13]

Olshansky himself acknowledged the legitimacy of comparing *House* with *Cranes*. After *Cranes*, he said, one must either 'work along the lines developed by the very talented people who made that film, or do something diametrically different'. He favors the latter, because in his view *Cranes* calculates its effects too much. 'It plainly illustrates the separation of form from content. Every frame cries out, "What a brilliant cameraman I am! What an inventive director I am!" ... Such artfulness, the studied quality [*narochitost'*] of the picture should, I think, have no place in and are alien to our film aesthetic.'[14]

Liudmila Pogozheva, editor of *Iskusstvo kino*, mildly objected to the lack of development in the heroes of *House*, who hardly change although nearly two decades, roughly a third of their lives, pass in the course of the film.[15] But she expressed a minority view. For much of the film industry establishment, *The House I Live in* had, thanks largely to Olshansky's script, successfully 'located and revealed' the poetry in everyday reality. Segel and Kulidzhanov had definitively articulated their point of view, and had found a cinematic medium for conveying an overwhelmingly important idea: that inner values and principles, not factory smokestacks or geological expeditions, define the essence of workers' lives.[16]

Audiences genuinely liked *The House I Live in*. It lacks the hallmarks of individual genius that are everywhere visible, for good and bad, in *The Cranes are Flying*. It offered admirable characters, intelligible motivations, affecting relationships; it echoed the prevailing partiality for prosaic cinema over poetic cinema. As one appreciative viewer commented at a discussion sponsored by the Academy of Sciences in early 1958, one cares about the characters in *House*, hence its superiority to *Cranes*. 'In *House*,' he added, distinguishing it from *Cranes*, 'I noticed neither the director nor the cameraman, but I saw people who remained with me ... The artists were able to create heroes they themselves loved, and they made us love them too.'[17]

No system, whether Hollywood's or the Kremlin's, favors idiosyncratic art over conventional, singular over replicable, unique over formulaic. While popular culture may occasionally take up and reward the unorthodox, it relies wholesale on formula. (Indeed, three decades later Vera Shitova described *House* as a forerunner of television serials.)[18] The official establishment could not and did not deny *Cranes'* significance – but it quite naturally preferred *House*.

Critical Responses, at Home and Abroad

The Cranes are Flying is a Soviet film, made first and foremost for Soviet viewers, and its intended audience responded to it warmly. After its release within the Soviet Union, *Cranes* moved abroad. The isolation of the Soviet film industry, as of the Soviet Union altogether, had begun to abate as soon as Stalin died. Previous Soviet movies had competed at foreign festivals, and a few (*The Big Family* among them) had won prizes, including secondary prizes at Cannes. But in 1957, although it hardly flung open its borders to foreigners (and KGB agents routinely disguised themselves as Intourist guides), the USSR took a major step in eliminating the Soviet Union's de facto cultural quarantine by hosting the International Youth Festival. Jazz and rock-and-roll competed with vapid Soviet popular songs and, among younger listeners, triumphed easily. Similar events and foreign exchanges followed, and in the spring of 1958, *Cranes* went to Cannes, accompanied by Urusevsky and Samoilova (Kalatozov was unable to join them).

Cranes had only one serious rival in the competition on aesthetic grounds, Jacques Tati's *Mon Oncle*. Sergei Iutkevich, a jury member in 1958 as he had been the year before, recalled that throughout the festival critics and audiences clearly favored *Cranes*. (He arranged a special screening to which Picasso and Jean Cocteau came; Picasso's praise especially pleased Urusevsky, and the two men met subsequently.) But the jury, not the public, chose the prize-winners, and the jury split. ('I was confident of the honesty of some members,' wrote Iutkevich, giving the word 'honesty' a particular spin, 'but there were others ... ') In 1958 the eleven-man jury consisted of four members from France and one each from Italy, the United States, West Germany, Japan, Great Britain, the Soviet Union and Spain (the last a Hungarian by birth).

Like the Nobel Committee and other prize-awarding bodies, Cannes juries did not ignore politics, though they naturally claimed to base their judgments exclusively on artistic merit. And two days before the festival officially closed and the jury bestowed its ribbons, politics intervened with a vengeance. After more than three years of tension between European Algerians and nationalist Muslim Algerians, with both sides engaging in violence, riots erupted on 13 May 1958. Thousands of European Algerians, unwilling to accept the control of the National Liberation Front, mobbed the offices of the governor-general. With the support of the military, they demanded the integration of Algeria with France, and called for power to be given to Charles de Gaulle. Consistent with its anti-colonialist stance, the Soviet Union had supported the Algerian nationalist independence movement, and condemned the putsch.

In that very tense atmosphere, when for a few weeks civil war seemed a real possibility, the Cannes jury deliberated. At first the French delegation nominated *Mon Oncle* for the Grand Prize, and nominated *Cranes* for a special jury award. In the first round of voting the Italian, German and American (and of course Soviet) delegates voted for *Cranes*, the Japanese, Spanish and British chose Tati's film, and the French delegation split: two voted for *Cranes*, two for *Mon Oncle*. Thus *Cranes* had a majority (six to five). But the chairman of the jury, that year the publisher Marcel Hachard, was entitled to cast two ballots, and he tied the vote by choosing the Tati film. (Iutkevich claims that a high official in the French Ministry of Foreign Affairs had phoned Hachard and informed him that it was 'undesirable' for a Soviet film to win the Grand Prize.)

Hachard solomonically proposed two grand prizes, one to each movie, an option Iutkevich categorically rebuffed. He lobbied hard among jury members, and after eight rounds of voting on whether or not to share the prize, the jury finally rejected that solution. Seven hours later, by secret ballot, the jury resolved to award *Cranes* the Golden Palm.[19] They gave Urusevsky the first prize for cinematography, and acknowledged Samoilova's performance with a 'special diploma'. (Samoilova's popularity continued in France, where she garnered other acting awards in 1958 and 1961.)[20]

On the other side of the Cold War divide, one disgruntled American journalist at Cannes reported that the prize to *Cranes* met with 'more resignation than enthusiasm'. The journalist, writing under the pseudonym 'Candor Rex', himself favored *Mon Oncle*: 'Russia's *When the Storks Fly Over* [sic] has such an obvious propaganda line one tends to forget it and concentrate on a love story considerably enhanced by a sloe-eyed beauty and intelligent actress ... ' (Apart from the title, presumably translated from the French, Candor Rex may have missed one or two of the film's subtleties. A few stills illustrate his article; one, showing Mark seated at the piano during the birthday party, is captioned: 'The brothel'.)[21]

Basking in the luster of the Cannes Golden Palm – the most prestigious of all film awards – the Soviet authorities entered *Cranes* in other international festivals, and authorized commercial distribution of *Cranes* abroad. The prizes awarded in Locarno, Vancouver and Mexico all denoted international recognition of the post-Stalinist Soviet Union; moreover, to a country as hungry for hard currency as it was for prestige, the film's international success meant significant box-office revenues.

Most Western critics reacted with more insight as well as more sympathy than Mr Rex. When *Cranes* opened in London in the autumn of 1958, the *Sunday Times* applauded its 'miraculous opening shots with their variety of planes and points of view', as well as its emotional scale.[22] The British Film Institute Bulletin ran a fair-minded, generally friendly review, calling the film

> a mixture, sometimes exhilarating, sometimes bizarre, of magazine story clichés, genuine lyricism and full-blooded virtuoso camerawork ... The characters are endowed with a humanity which allows the heroine to be weak and the villain to claim some of our sympathy; even so, such details as the implication that it takes an artist to be a coward and the absurd overpainting of the scenes of dissolution in wartime Siberia often make the script seem crude by Western standards ...

Like nearly everyone, this reviewer acclaimed Samoilova without reservation, regarding her acting as the 'centrepiece' of the film.

> Her great achievement has been to fashion out of indifferent material a clear and touching personality, which seems to have one dimension more than any other character in the story. She is given every help by an adoring camera; the photography, indeed, is the second star of the film – at its worst ostentatious and flamboyant, at its best, unobtrusively elastic and lucid.[23]

In France *Cranes* became a major box-office hit, attracting viewers in numbers then unprecedented for a Soviet film and never again matched: nearly five and a half million viewers saw it during its initial commercial run.[24] Like their British colleagues, reviewers in *L'Express* and *Libération*, two moderately left-wing periodicals, drew attention to Urusevsky's lyrical camera and to Samoilova's skill; the *Libération* critic approvingly contrasted Samoilova's purity and authenticity with that Western female icon, Brigitte Bardot. A Polish film journal made the same point, differentiating Veronika – awkward, lacking coquetry, inarticulate – from Western screen sexpots. If Rita Hayward and Marilyn Monroe create exceptional types on screen, images of femininity inaccessible to ordinary women, Samoilova plays Veronika as the opposite, a girl similar to millions of girls, though one poetically exaggerated.[25] Samoilova herself recalled a gift she received at an East German film festival, a watch with the poignant (and lengthy!) inscription: 'Finally we see on the Soviet screen a face, not a mask.'[26]

Cranes played in theaters in Western and Eastern Europe, in Latin America and in parts of Asia, in 1958, and cinema-goers – even discounting the obvious bombast – apparently agreed with the critics: *Cranes* had audiences weeping in France (*Journal de Dimanche*) and on their feet applauding in Mexico (*Noticias*); it inspired Bulgarians to become 'better and more humane', Romanians and Japanese to hate war.[27]

Viewers in the United States waited more than a year before they could see *Cranes*. Warner Brothers, its distributors, released it in late 1959, 'timorously [inserting] a blurb at the beginning of the film which absolved them from responsibility should any American become tainted with the Soviet ideologies which surely must be lurking *somewhere* behind the innnocent façade of a love story'.[28] (They also listed Urusevsky's name as 'Serge Uresovsky'.) Writing in a journal for cinephiles, who might be presumed to have some (unhappy) familiarity with Soviet pictures from an earlier era, the reviewer continues: 'This bit of patriotism does the film a disservice. It tends to put one off; it creates the possibility, at the onset at least, that we are about to see one of those dreadful Stalinist happy-tractor films of the *genre* of *Cossacks of the Kuban*.'[29]

Samoilova's acting and Urusevsky's artistry particularly impressed both Mitchell Lifton (writing in *Film Quarterly*) and Bosley Crowther in the *New York Times*. The former considered *Cranes* 'a film which, in the skill of its direction, in the verve of its camerawork and editing, and in the unified virtuosity of its acting, deserves to be spoken of in the company of such films as *The Seventh Seal* and *Miss Julie*'. Crowther, more moderate, praised Batalov's Boris as 'a pleasant and credible young man moved by romantic impulses and shattered by fates outside himself' and Samoilova's 'excellent performance as ... a fine, fecund-looking young woman torn from her lover by the war'. He recognized Kalatozov's cinematic roots in the 'heroic revolutionary' tradition of Pudovkin and Dovzhenko. 'But M. Kalatozov has brought it up to date to blend with sound and the overlapping idioms of modern screen reportage. It might also be called neo-romanticism, applied to a tragic tale.'[30]

These two critics, like other American reviewers and far more than their European counterparts, seemed to scrutinize *Cranes* for its propaganda potential.[31] Crowther speculates that 'deliberate propaganda aims' inhere in the grandmother's leave-taking of Boris, when she makes the sign of the cross over him, and in the visibility of Mark's brand of piano, a Steinway. Presumably the latter identifies Mark with the German enemy; the political import of the former eludes me, but perhaps Crowther takes it as an intimation of the state's religious forbearance.

For Crowther, Veronika's marriage, however expedient as the basis for her later despair and repentance, lacks logic, 'is the most glaring fault of the plot', and 'represents a conspicuous old-fashioned romantic cliché'. (He reduces the complexity of *Cranes* to 'a fable', the moral of which 'is that one should stay faithful to one's love'.) Lifton concurred: 'For some reason which remains unclear but which must involve Soviet ethics, she decides to marry him ... ' Yet despite the banality of the plot, Lifton wrote, 'the film treads a thin and careful line between bathos and sincerity, between the banality of overstated, unwarranted sentiment, and the stark, absurd, recognizable simplicity of a real and common experience. The plot, when abstracted and set down, becomes insufferably simplistic; it is the *film's* great achievement that it never becomes so.'

Although Lifton misunderstands bits of *Cranes*' story (for instance, he mistakes Fiodor Ivanovich and Veronika in the final scene for father and daughter), he analyzes the style of *Cranes* with a good deal of sophistication and subtlety:

Two styles – one a very straight, naturalistic, pictorial rendering, the other a fast, nervous, symbolized evocation – seem to be in constant conflict throughout the film. What begins as a highly stylized visual convention suddenly turns into a very naturalistic one, and when we have become used to that, reverses itself again; the *adagio* of realism is reinvested with new meaning by the *allegro* of the montage scenes. What makes this apparent hodge-podge work is the fact that these movements, to extend the musical analogy, are both based on the same themes. A unity accrues which is not one of continuity but of rhythm, of the repetition and elaboration of certain symbolic elements, and of the way in which the camera treats these elements.[32]

Notes

1. RGALI Fond 2453, delo 620.
2. R. Iurenev, 'Vernost'', *Iskusstvo kino* 12 (1957), p. 10.
3. Aleksandr Zarkhi, *O samom glavnom: zametki kinorezhissera* (Moscow, 1964), pp. 3–10 passim. This particular essay was published seven years after *Cranes*' release, in a time of new cultural retrenchment, but Zarkhi expressed such views more than once.
4. Maia Turovskaia, '"Da" i "net"', *Iskusstvo kino* 12 (1957), p. 17.
5. R. Messer, 'Molodye o molodykh', in *Molodye rezhissery sovetskogo kino* (Moscow, 1962), p. 21.
6. I. Shneiderman, 'V poiskakh stilia', in *Molodye rezhissery sovetskogo kino*, pp. 219–22 passim.
7. Dmitry and Vladimir Shlapentokh, *Soviet Cinematography 1918–1991* (New York, 1993), p. 138.
8. Shneiderman, 'V poiskakh ... ', (p. 222) and Messer 'Molodye ... ' (p. 22) both cite Seriozha's speech as the credo of Soviet youth, 'a living ideal they wish to emulate'. Two years later, however, it was deemed too abstract and ahistorical. A man can discover bauxite and oil, 'but if he takes a neutral stance towards the life and death issues of his country', he forfeits the sympathy of audiences. F. Khodzhaev, 'My ishchem geroia', *Iskusstvo kino* 1 (1959), p. 59.
9. Shneiderman, 'V poiskakh ... ', p. 216.
10. RGALI Fond 2468, op. 2, delo 208: 2–3.
11. Ibid., p. 15.
12. Ibid., pp. 23–5 passim.
13. Ibid., p. 31.
14. Ibid., pp. 36–7.
15. L. Pogozheva, 'Dom, v kotorom ia zhivu: Obsuzhdenie fil'ma v sektore kino Instituta istorii iskusstv AN SSSR', *Iskusstvo kino* 2 (1958), pp. 88–9.

16. K. Paramonova and S. Freilikh, in ibid., p. 85 and p. 86 respectively.
17. S. Ginzburg, 'Bez vneshnykh èffektov', in ibid., p. 91.
18. Cited in Sergei Zemlianukhin and Miroslava Segida, *Domashniaia sinemateka: otechestvennoe kino 1918–1996* (Moscow, 1996), p. 128.
19. Sergei Iutkevich, 'Kann, 1958 god ... ' in 'Portrety', *Iskusstvo kino* 3 (1980), pp. 102–7 passim.
20. See the report on the competition results submitted to the Central Committee by then Minister of Culture Mikhailov, in V. Fomin (ed.), *Kinematograf ottepeli: Dokumenty i svidetel'stva* (Moscow, 1998), pp. 363–4.
21. Candor Rex, 'Cannes 1958', *Films in Review* ix, 6 (June–July 1958), pp. 290–5 passim.
22. *Sunday Times*, 14 September 1958.
23. K.C., *BFI Monthly Film Bulletin*, October 1958, p. 125. In the same issue 'J.G.' reviews another Soviet production, Sergei Gerasimov's adaptation of *And Quiet Flows the Don* [Tikhii Don], also quite sympathetically and sensitively.
24. S. V. Kudriavtsev, *Vse – kino*, cited by Zemlianukhin and Segida, *Domashniaia* ... , p. 227.
25. Cited in L.N. Poznanskaia (ed.), *Letiat zhuravli* (Moscow, 1972), pp. 146–7.
26. Tat'iana Samoilova, 'Èto bylo moe ... .' *Kinovedcheskie zapiski* 17 (1993), p. 47.
27. For a sampling of excerpts, see Iurii Bogomolov, *Mikhail Kalatozov: Stranitsy tvorcheskoi biografii* (Moscow, 1989), pp. 162–3 and Pogozheva, 'Dom ... ', pp. 145–9.
28. Mitchell Lifton, '*The Cranes are Flying*', *Film Quarterly* xiii, 3 (Spring 1960) (University of California Press, Berkeley), p. 42.
29. Richard Stites calls Ivan Pyrev's 1949 romantic comedy about the love between two collective farm directors, 'the ultimate glossy film, released at a time of severe shortages and the ravages of recovery ... From the opening chorus amid fields of grain to the fairbooths bulging with melons, bikes, books, and shoes, *Cossacks* mystified the economic life of rural Russia. When young Mikhail Gorbachev saw it in the early 1950s, he said to his companion: "It's not like that at all."' Richard Stites, *Russian Popular Culture: Entertainment and Society Since 1900* (Cambridge, 1992), p. 121.
30. Bosley Crowther, 'The Cranes are Flying', *New York Times*, 22 March 1960, 31, p. 2.
31. See reviews in *Commonweal* (18 December 1959), *The Nation* (9 April 1960), *New Yorker* (2 April 1960), *Newsweek* (7 December 1959) and *Time* (22 February 1960).
32. Lifton, '*The Cranes* ... ', p. 43.

5. Aftermath

Film Establishment

Within the Soviet Union, *Cranes* continued to occupy a canonical place in Soviet cinema, albeit a double-edged one. A few years after its release Sergei Gerasimov reaffirmed its importance. He recalled how its 'muscular energy had supplanted sleepy inertia, its dynamic expressiveness had replaced vague muttering ... It could not help but agitate and arouse hopes for the future. And young people understood this with special acuteness, immediately linking the film's ideas with its aesthetic innovations.'[1]

Fair enough. Yet Gerasimov's accolade served as the means towards an unpleasant end: to set up (and justify) an attack on another film. In this case the tactic – well-worn in Soviet cultural history – proposed to disparage Tengiz Abuladze's *Someone Else's Children* [Chuzhie deti, 1958], a beautifully observed psychological drama about a woman who marries a man she doesn't love for the sake of his children, and stays with them when he abandons her for a new lover. More than once, through neither fault nor merit of its own, *Cranes* became a stick with which members of the cinema establishment, as well as more unambiguously official spokesmen of the state, could beat controversial films. The attacks usually took the form of congratulating *Cranes* on its scale [*masshtabnost'*, a favorite desideratum] and castigating the targeted film for its hermeticism, its narrow focus, its trifling concerns.

Thus Gerasimov, having established *Cranes' bona fides*, proceeded to lambast the newer film that fails to live up to the standards set by *Cranes*. He harshly spurned as 'either entirely naïve or unreliable' the film-maker who feels no need to 'articulate his political credo', who uses his talent as a 'shield against reality and against criticism'. Such directors can always count on an audience, given the endless supply of 'Tartuffes', egotists and philistines who prefer stale melodramas to fresh socially committed work, and of pretentious aesthetes, who 'cover yawns when social conflict appears on screen, and who regard our socialist world as secondary to new language and terminology'.

Abuladze's film appeals to the latter. It offers, Gerasimov conceded, a certain negligible veracity [*malen'kaia pravda*]: namely, that people are more alike than they are different. But 'people of the Soviet socialist world fortunately do *not* resemble their forebears, though they carry the heavy burden inherited from the base old world'. Abuladze's film exposes the director's own failure to understand the 'new socialist world', and serves in turn as a litmus test of the viewer's moral health or weakness, depending on his reaction.[2]

Cranes was not alone in being used punitively. Two other war films joined it in a triad of commercially and critically successful war pictures: Sergei Bondarchuk's *The Fate of a Man* [Sud'ba cheloveka], released early in 1959, and Grigori Chukhrai's *Ballad of a Soldier* [Ballada o soldate], released at the tail end of the same year. Bondarchuk based his film on a story written by Mikhail Sholokhov in 1946, though published only in 1956, when the thaw sanctioned its apolitical patriotism. Its hero, Andrei Sokolov (Bondarchuk), manages to escape from a Nazi POW camp, bringing back to Soviet lines valuable booty: a German major with a briefcase full of precious information. A German bomb kills Sokolov's wife and two daughters; his son perishes at the front, literally on the eve of victory. After the war Sokolov meets up with an orphan, and they form a new 'family'.

Critics interpreted *Fate of a Man* as successor to classic Soviet films. Sokolov became the godchild of heroes like Maxim, Chapaev and – gender difference notwithstanding – Alexandra Sokolova, the heroine of Kheifits and Zarkhi's 1940 *Member of the Government*. They compared *Fate of a Man* favorably with Andrzej Munk's 'near-slanderous' film about Polish prisoners-of-war, *Eroica* [Poland, 1958]. In this ideologized reading of the film, Sokolov derives the strength to survive from having the 'character, world-view, and morality of a Russian, a Soviet man'.[3] In fact Sokolov hardly resembles Chapaev. His tragedies have damaged him irreparably. He survives, and somehow retains the capacity to love, as demonstrated by the bond he forms with his adopted son, but his heart is broken and he fears for his little son's future should it stop altogether.

Furthermore, Bondarchuk repeatedly minimizes the 'heroic' or 'exceptional' dimension of his hero's actions, whereas the opposite is true of *Chapaev* and the Maxim trilogy. When the Russian PoWs are barracked in a ruined church, Sokolov overhears one prisoner matter-of-factly express his intention of divulging to the Germans the Party affiliation of another prisoner, information that would ensure the latter's death. With the Party man's help, Sokolov strangles the would-be informer. Necessary the silent execution may be; heroic it is decidedly not. Bondarchuk similarly downplays the hazards of Sokolov's journey when he escapes with his captive major, skipping over the dangerous encounters to cut straight to their arrival behind Soviet lines.

Chukhrai expresses an analogous vision in *Ballad*, insisting that a man's essence reveals itself in the unexceptional, not the exceptional. Chukhrai structured *Ballad* as an extended flashback, beginning and ending with a grieving woman standing on a road, fields and forests behind her. The flashback framework emphasizes war as a fatal irruption into ordinary life; the body of the film concentrates on the 'normal', even if that normalcy exists within an alien and abnormal state of war.

In the opening sequence, the only 'battle scene' of the film, nineteen-year-old Aliosha Skvortsov flees in panic before he shoots at and disables two German tanks. Rewarded with a week's leave, Aliosha heads home to help his mother repair the roof, but he exhausts almost the entire leave helping others. He barely has time to embrace his mother before he turns back, to the front and to his death. Aliosha's heroism manifests itself precisely in the unexceptional context, and the individuals he encounters are mainly civilians whose heroism plays out in prosaic, quotidian reality far from the front.

Not everyone appreciated this aspect of *Ballad*. The studio initially considered *Ballad*'s script too 'ordinary', and Chukhrai was advised to give Shura, the young girl who joins Aliosha on the train, an 'exploit' comparable to Aliosha's tank maneuver.⁴ On the eve of *Ballad of a Soldier*'s commercial release, dubious theater managers in Leningrad's best cinemas substituted *Room at the Top* [Put' v vysshee obshchestvo], thinking it more 'reliable'.⁵

Once released, *Ballad* quickly won over viewers. Yet like other war films of the time, *Ballad of a Soldier* required justification because it ignored 'contemporary life'. Stanislav Rostotsky acquitted the film on the (rather far-fetched) basis of its edifying nature: 'Workers in the arts should think of the souls and hearts of the generation who were children [during the war], to concern themselves with their education ... [Chukhrai] wants the radiant memory of people like Skvortsov to help today's world and to illuminate the future ... '⁶ A colleague valued Aliosha's 'Soviet' character, which 'could not have been forged in the atmosphere of an orangerie or a hothouse', presumably found only in the West. Aliosha is 'our contemporary' because 'in the moment before his death [a moment not actually shown in the film – JW] he turned his face toward the future, and his eyes glowed with the reflected light of the morrow'.⁷

Such praise seems curiously unsuitable for *Ballad*, and indeed, most critics, at home and abroad, celebrated in Chukhrai's film the qualities that still affect audiences: its simplicity, the goodness of nearly all the characters, the film's organic, natural flow, violated only by the 'overly explicit' image of heroism presented when Aliosha tries to help the survivors of a bombed trainload of refugees.⁸ At Cannes, *Ballad* contrasted appealingly with Antonioni and Buñuel's surrealism, and with Fellini's scandal-provoking *La Dolce Vita* (which nevertheless won the Golden Palm). The British press called it a 'calming note in a discordant symphony'; *Le Monde* acknowledged that 'from time to time it's nice to see normal and healthy people on screen'.⁹

Ballad of a Soldier exploits the 'journey' motif, that voyage of the soul reified in physical movement. Figures appear and disappear, but the journey continues, giving the film its unity and its rhythm. 'Aliosha Skvortsov's road to his native village becomes his road to himself,' wrote Maia Turovskaia. He truly wishes to get home, so that his reluctance at every turning point testifies that real choice is involved, but each time he chooses the kind, the decent, the noble alternative. *Ballad* lacks invention; it is driven by the immutability of a fairy tale's moral law, where 'beauty equals happiness and ugliness unhappiness, where the hero never fails to help the helpless and never errs, precisely thanks to his naïveté'.[10]

Ballad continued the ongoing transformation of the heroic concept in Soviet cinema. Its opening sequence, when Aliosha flees from the advancing tank and then, burrowed into the ground, fires at it in blind dread, is 'a plainly ironic attack on the established traditions of front-line heroism'.[11] As in *Fate*, no single brilliant feat constitutes heroism in *Ballad*. Rather, many separate details constitute the heroic mosaic, each mini-story a variation on the initial theme: Aliosha defies a greedy sentry on the train, helps a one-legged soldier with his gear, brings soap to a soldier's unfaithful wife and then takes it to a worthier recipient, the soldier's bedridden father.[12] But the rhythmic repetition of the theme penetrates our minds with the power of what Eisenstein called 'shamanic incantation'.[13] Aliosha Skvortsov does not have to make one fateful choice on which his future depends. He must make many small choices, none of them decisive, most of them inconsequential. Yet, unlike Veronika, who for much of *Cranes* remains the passive victim of fate, Aliosha consistently acts. And what would be admirable as a single week's worth of actions becomes something much greater, because the prefatory voiceover has told us that it is Aliosha's last week of such actions: he will have no more of them.

At the turn of the decade a contradictory mood pervaded the Soviet Union, with discrepant signals characterizing both politics and culture. Economic and social gains at home vied with increased tension between the USSR and China and – after the U-2 incident of May 1960 – with the United States. The official media barely acknowledged Boris Pasternak's death, but within weeks the KGB arrested his mistress and her daughter, convicting them for supposed currency speculations and sentencing them to terms in labor camps. On the one hand the authorities endorsed the publication of controversial texts like Ilia Ehrenburg's memoirs and Konstantin Simonov's war novel, *The Living and the Dead* [Zhivye i mertvye]. On the other hand, a controversial literary anthology, *Pages from Tarusa* [Tarusskie stranitsy], appeared in a substantial print-run (75,000), only to disappear from sale almost immediately; the ban lasted until 1962.

In the increasingly confrontational atmosphere of 1959–61, *Cranes*,

Fate of a Man and *Ballad of a Soldier* – whatever their separate and collective virtues – became stalking-horses for officials who wished to ambush more problematic films. One such was Marlen Khutsiev's *Two Fiodors* [*Dva Fedora*, 1958], set in the immediately post-war period. Khutsiev's film opens with a troop train returning home from the front in a complex aural and visual montage (shot by Peter Todorovsky) that owes much to *Cranes*. Adhering to a traditional pattern (men who 'mother' a child), 'Big' Fiodor (Vasily Shukshin) adopts Little Fiodor, a war orphan. (In an echo of Veronika's exchange with Borka, Big Fiodor asks 'Whose child are you?' [*Ty malyi chei?*], to which Little Fiodor replies, 'Nobody's' [*Nichei*].) But for the best part of the film, as they attempt to reconstruct their lives, it is not clear who is parenting whom. The two Fiodors look after each other, closer to two peers than to adult and child.

In autumn 1956, when Khutsiev first submitted the script, the studio had welcomed it. Then came the Hungarian revolt, and by the time he shot the film 'there were objections to anything "dark"'.[14] As happened frequently, the film itself had not changed so much as the times had. At the Kiev Ministry of Culture discussion verged on the ludicrous: 'The picture does not depict our reality, it is pessimistic and uninspiring. You can't tell what country it's set in. If it's ours, then why don't the school children wear red ties? And what sort of hero is this – sullen, taciturn, unsociable. That's not what our people are like. [*Razve nash chelovek takoi?*]'[15]

Most of *Two Fiodors* avoids conventional sentimentality. Unlike *Fate of a Man*, where Sokolov's emotion-laden flashbacks recall components of pre-war happiness such as his courtship of his wife and the birth and progress of his children, *Two Fiodors* neither tells nor shows us what either protagonist lost because of the war; it simply implies that both have lost everything.

Moreover, the alliance between the two resembles 'the ascetic bachelor friendship of two men, two soldiers'[16] more than it does a father–son bond, at least initially. Little Fiodor lacks the patent vulnerability of Vania, the urchin Sokolov adopts. And although much of his bravado is for show, this tough and wary pragmatist knows – much better than the romantic Big Fiodor – how to scrounge scarce goods, and how to push past a line of people waiting to buy food. The coincidence of their names amazes the man ('Just think of it!');

the boy reacts matter-of-factly ('Well, it happens').[17] The diminutive nickname Fedia is reserved for Big, not Little Fiodor.

The role reversal (which involves its own kind of sentimentality) results from the difference in their war experiences. The child has better survival skills than the adult because war forced him to be self-reliant and taught him how. *Two Fiodors* represents peace as chaotic and unsettling for soldiers used to the structure, order, material provisions and support of army life. Amid post-war turmoil and scarcity these young men had no one to depend on except themselves.

Viktor Nekrasov, one of *Two Fiodors*' most eloquent defenders, wrote of the generation that left its school benches for the front and returned home to ashes: no house, no family, no friends. Though he carefully, explicitly, denied parallels with the West's 'lost generation' ('We had and have no such lost generation'), he in fact described its Soviet counterpart: boys who learned 'two skills in their seventeen to eighteen years – how to kill and how not to be killed. And how are they to live now, when such skills are not needed?'[18]

The state could not and did not accept Khutsiev's radical revision of the peacetime experience, rejecteding it with commensurate anger. With the temper of the times demanding conspicuous heroism on a large scale, *Two Fiodors* provided an easy target. Khutsiev's heroes may be 'very dear' people, Iakov Varshavsky grudgingly admitted, but they lead 'circumscribed lives'; the film fails to furnish the moral armaments needed to conquer the 'fronts' of life. 'We are sure', Varshavsky wrote,

> that not long before the action of the film, Fiodor himself lived, thought, felt on a 'high note', because he felt responsible for the whole country. But the film-makers chose to present this powerful epic image of the master of the nation from a different point of view. If we can believe them, Fiodor in peacetime is not the same man as he was in wartime ... [He] shows no interest in the country, in the world ...[19]

Another critic wondered whether the heroes, as they rebuild their house, have in mind the house 'of simple Soviet people, connected to the whole huge nation by a thousand threads', or the bourgeois concept of 'my home as my castle'.[20]

Throughout the 1960s, *Cranes, Ballad of a Soldier* and *Fate of a Man* served as weapons in various domestic ideological and cultural battles. The staunch conservative Vadim Baskakov, deputy director of Goskino and then director of the All-Union Scientific Research Institute of Film Art (VNIIK), wielded them against films anathematized as 'naturalistic' and 'pacifist', such as Alov and Naumov's *Peace to Him Who Enters* [Mir vkhodiashchemu, 1961]: the former inspire viewers with 'faith in ideals', he wrote, while the latter corrode such faith; the former reveal 'the truth of history', while the latter distort that truth.[21] Another film industry bureaucrat, Mikhail Kuznetsov, concurred: in *Cranes*, even during the battlefront sequence, man is not 'a slave of circumstance, as the naturalists would have it; amid the bitterness and gloom of the war strides the Soviet soldier'.[22]

As ever in the Soviet Union, where a single matrix embraced art and ideology, such debates involved political shifts more than they involved art; doctrinal deviations, career advancement and public access mattered more than the powerful influence of Kalatozov and Urusevsky's aesthetic and thematic choices. But outside of official circles, fellow film-makers, especially younger colleagues, scrutinized *Cranes* with professional eyes, and drew their own conclusions.

Transition

Vadim Iusov, a recent graduate of the State Institute of Cinematography (VGIK) in 1957, recalled the impact of *Cranes*: 'The long-shots, the hand-held camera were revolutionary in those years when camerawork still tended to be static, as were the use of crane shots, the long-focus optics, in order to convey feeling and ideas (not simply for the sake of showing off).' Urusevsky, although a man then in his fifties, had imbued *Cranes* with the expressiveness and the emotional passion of a young man.[23]

Others of Iusov's generation agreed. Gennadi Shpalikov was a young screenwriter at the time. His scripts – for Khutsiev's ill-fated *Ilyich's Gate* [Zastava Il'icha, 1961; rel. 1965 as *I am Twenty*, Mne dvadtsat' let], for Danelia's *I Stroll Around Moscow* [Ia shagaiu po Moskve, 1963, which Shpalikov co-directed], and for his own *A Long and Happy Life* [Dolgaia schastlivaia zhizn', 1967] – would capture with uncommon exactness the language, behavior and *Zeitgeist* of his contemporaries. Shpalikov remembered his initial reaction to *Cranes*:

'My story is a simple one. Back then, in 1957, I had never known or seen anything better, and what's more, I never wanted to.'[24]

Urusevsky destroyed the barrier between spectator and scene, an innovation as revolutionary as the removal of the stage curtain in the theater.[25] Mark Zak, a cinema historian and scholar not yet thirty when *Cranes* opened, recalled his astonishment at *Cranes*' 'visual plasticity' and montage, reminiscent as they were of silent cinema. He found its visuality particularly remarkable given the film's roots in the essentially verbal literary medium of drama.[26]

Often, cinematographers copied Urusevsky's techniques and effects without understanding their underlying logic. 'After *Cranes*,' Semion Freilikh complained, people began to speak about

> Urusevsky's 'subjective camera'. So many imitators appeared, we saw so many distorted frames and swirling birches on screen, as if that were the essence of Urusevsky's vision, as if the same Urusevsky had not shot – and shot calmly, objectively and unemotionally – *Cavalier of the Golden Star* a few year earlier. His camera became emotional and subjective when it had to, to discern and reveal Veronika.[27]

It remained subjective in the next Kalatozov–Urusevsky collaboration, the passionately anticipated *Unsent Letter*. Audiences, critics, filmmakers and officials predicted and awaited another triumph. European distributors were so confident that they signed contracts for the new film sight unseen,[28] especially since *The Unsent Letter*, based on a story by Valeri Osipov, brought together many of the same people who had worked on *Cranes*. Kalatozov directed, Urusevsky manned the camera, Rozov worked on the script (together with Grigori Koltunov and Osipov), and the 'new idol' Tatiana Samoilova starred, along with two of the Soviet Union's most popular male actors: Innokenti Smoktunovsky and Evgeni Urbansky. (A third, Vasili Livanov, began a successful career with *The Unsent Letter*.)

The Unsent Letter depicts a geological expedition seeking diamonds in the Siberian taiga. It at once exemplified and significantly departed from the 'geology epidemic' then sweeping the Soviet cultural scene. Young writers (including Osipov) whose work appeared in the popular journal *Iunost* turned eagerly to the location and to the vocation, fraught as they both were with palpable and easily comprehensible hardships and rewards. Artists romanticized the taiga as a prelapsarian Eden, where betrayal had no place and one could be natural and true to oneself. As one popular song went, 'Stand firm, geologist, be strong, geologist, you are brother to the wind and sun' [*Derzhis', geolog, krepis', geolog, ty vetru i solntsu brat*].[29]

In *The Unsent Letter* disasters befall and destroy the expedition members after they find the diamonds and start their return journey. Urbansky's character, the guide Sergei, hopelessly in love with Samoilova's Tania, perishes in a raging fire. Livanov's Andrei, loving and loved by Tania, becomes so feeble that he removes himself, going off alone into the taiga to ensure the other two a better chance to survive. Despite his self-sacrifice, Tania dies as well. The last of the four, Smoktunovsky's Sabinin, leader of the expedition, manages to reach the ice-filled river, where he lashes together a raft on which he floats downstream. Starving, and clutching to his breast both the 'unsent letter' of the title and a map of the diamond deposits, he weakly motions with his hands. The circling, searching helicopter catches sight of his signal, and rescues the precious map and its guardian. (In the first version of the film Sabinin is already dead when the helicopter reaches him. The studio editors and censors required a brief prolongation of life, so that he could be alive when found – but he does not last long).[30]

Soviet movie fans intently followed the adventures of the shooting crew, which set off for Siberia with elaborate paraphernalia and equipment, in order to – as one participant recalled – create a taiga within the taiga. Kalatozov and Urusevsky took real risks as they filmed; so did the cast. The fire that killed Urbansky's Sergei actually burned Samoilova; Smoktunovsky, though swathed in special protective gear, nearly froze on the ice floe. The line between art and life seemed permeable, the cast and crew as heroic as the characters.

The Unsent Letter probably could not have fulfilled the hypertrophied expectations of its audience: they awaited not merely a movie, but a transformative experience such as *Cranes* had provided. The film that opened puzzled and dismayed them. The conflict within *The Unsent Letter* occurs outside of human consciousness, between man and nature, competing forces so unevenly matched that audiences felt as irrelevant as the characters. As a Georgian reviewer sadly concluded, 'With all its cinematic brilliance, the picture resembles its cold sun, blindingly radiant but with no power to warm.'[31]

Most critics at the time identified as the source of the film's failure its awkward amalgamation of two strands. One was a conventional psychological drama, complete with romantic triangle (and fisticuffs between Sergei and Andrei) and Sabinin's faithful wife waiting for him at home. The other consisted of what Lev Anninsky called 'symbolic frescos' about people and nature, where the film's cinematography displaces in importance its human drama.[32] The *dramatis personae*, despite the charisma of all four stars, remain unpersuasive.

The Unsent Letter met official – as opposed to popular and critical – disapproval because it inverted the proclaimed values of the sputnik era, when official iconography presented man and cosmos as a unified whole. Should a conflict between the two arise, man must inevitably dominate. *The Unsent Letter* begins as a familiar anthem to Soviet man's struggle with – and, by customary implication, victory over – implacable nature. But it departs from the formula, and shows nature wholly indifferent to human beings, their claims to supremacy notwithstanding.[33] Indeed, a few years later, when conservatives attacked Mikhail Romm's *Nine Days of a Year* [Deviat' dnei odnogo goda, 1962], they emphasized precisely that genealogy: *Cranes*, with its 'fall of a hopeless philistine unable to remain faithful', and *The Unsent Letter*, where man's doomed struggle with nature is 'completely alien to socialist humanism', had spawned the malignancy of Romm's new picture.[34]

From today's vantage point, the film appears to bid farewell to the utopian Soviet view of man as center of the universe: instead, in *The Unsent Letter*, he literally loses the ground from under his feet. Nature's eye – to borrow Evgeni Margolit's apt term – becomes the controlling and normal point of view, cinematically; human vision is skewed. When characters gaze out at the overwhelming landscape, the camera foreshortens what they see, suggesting their disorientation and insecurity. Conversely, when nature regards (as it were) the characters, the shot straightens out and regains stability. Nature's eye is level, calm and uninvolved.

The profoundly individual vision of Kalatozov and Urusevsky, most perfectly realized in *Cranes*, less successfully in *The Unsent Letter* (and their final collaboration, the 1964 *I am Cuba*), invigorated subsequent Soviet cinema. Examples of imitation abound, as Freilikh grumbled. But so do more significant examples of original growth spurred by Kalatozov and Urusevsky's work. The wealth of faces Kalatozov and Urusevsky unveiled, the psychological states Urusevsky's camera movement created as much as it captured, and the freedom and naturalness of behavior on screen for the first time in *Cranes*, reappear more than once, perhaps most dramatically in Marlen Khutsiev's *Ilyich's Gate*, a film in many other respects quite different. Like Kalatozov and Urusevsky, Khutsiev and his gifted cinematographer Margarita Pilikhina manipulate camera movement and distance, especially in filming crowd scenes, to suggest with great subtlety the relationship between the individual and the group. In the May Day parade that climaxes the first part of the film, for instance, one of the three young heroes of *Ilyich's Gate* pushes – like Veronika in the *provody*, and initially in the victory scene – through an enormous throng of people in pursuit of Ania, the girl he has fallen for; unlike Veronika until the very end of *Cranes*, he moves *with* the jubilant stream, his movement parallel to and energized by the pulsing host.

The structural climax of the second part of the film, a poetry reading at the Moscow Polytechnic Museum, replicates that paradox: Sergei has to push his way through mobs of eager listeners to reach Ania, who is already seated, but the nearly solid wall of human bodies his movements encounter supports rather than opposes him. Pilikhina's camera brilliantly captured the almost exalted mood of the reading, which was specifically organized for the film, but which differed in no way from the many actual readings of 1961 and 1962. Khutsiev later commented that Pilikhina's camera 'dived and swooped' as if echoing the rhythm and movement of the poetic lines.[35] The camera pans rapt faces, follows the request notes passed from the auditorium to the floor. The sequence looks spontaneous as well as authentic, as real as the documentary footage of the May Day parade. Indeed, as with the filming of *The Unsent Letter*, life and art blurred: the actors in *Ilyich's Gate* had to elbow their way into the hall through the crowd outside the door, and members of the audience protested that the film equipment obstructed their view of the poets (Yevtushenko, Boris Slutsky, Robert Rozhdestvensky, Bella Akhmadulina, Bulat Okudzhava and others).[36]

Thematically *Ilyich's Gate* moves in the opposite direction from *Cranes*. Although it begins by celebrating the individual's union with his society, with the Soviet utopia, it continues by representing the detailed process of departure from that utopia. Nevertheless, it bears the imprint of *Cranes*, as do so many films made in *Cranes*' wake, if only because *Cranes* validated all personal artistic vision, whether sharing Kalatozov and Urusevsky's particular style and ideas or not.

Influence

In the 1960s Soviet cinema moved in two complementary though seemingly contradictory directions at once: toward a cinema of 'documentality' and realism, among its highlights Iuli Raizman's *And What If It's Love?* [A esli èto liubov?, 1962], and Andrei Mikhalkov-Konchalovsky's *First Teacher* [Pervyi uchitel', 1966], and toward a 'poetic' cinema, perhaps best exemplified by *Ivan's Childhood* [Ivanovo detstvo, 1961] and the films coming out of Moldavian, Lithuanian, Ukrainian and Georgian studios slightly later. It is only a slight exaggeration to say that both trends had their roots in *Cranes*, because documentation became an act of individual artistic creativity, not a representation but a creation of the subject being documented. The 'documenting of external environment yielded to the documenting of personal perception and apprehension' of that environment.[37]

The advocates of documentarity wanted to create the illusion of life, of 'unadorned reality', on screen, and most often attempted to achieve that illusion by means of transparent or invisible artistic devices. Black-and-white served as one such device. Mikhalkov-Konchalovsky, in *First Teacher*, and even more in his second film, *The Story of How Asia Kliachina Loved but Did not Marry* [Istoriia Asi Kliachinoi, kotoraia liubila da ne vyshla zamuzh, 1966], relied on black-and-white to juxtapose as equals the world of reality (via improvised dialogue and casting of non-professionals) and the world of fiction. The camera's point of view mimics normal vision, eyeing what is close at hand, glancing under the table, peering into the distance. For him, black-and-white 'excludes external beauty as superfluous, inappropriate for the parable composition; it avoids the colored grandeur of nature, the unavoidable adornment of made-up faces. It focuses attention instead on the ... modest, unobtrusive authenticity of the image.'[38] When Andrei Tarkovsky chose black-and-white for *Andrei Rublev* (1966, rel. 1971), reserving color for the last stunning frames of Rublev's own icons, he struck a blow against the tradition of historical films 'doomed' to color, picturesqe museum replicas with holiday costumes and antique furniture. The documentary orientation manifested itself in every aspect of film-making. In terms of dramatic structure, plot receded into the background, replaced by the 'capricious movement' of life. Frame composition tried above all to capture that movement, with all its lack of premeditation and plan, and tried to make spontaneity the basis of the image system. In acting, the 'non-professional', 'natural' man (perhaps best embodied by Smoktunovsky) became the ideal.[39] 'Every shot should be seen as a piece of living reality,' said Mikhalkov-Konchalovsky. 'Ideally the film should look as if it has been edited from documentary footage which the director didn't shoot himself.'[40] The words might have been uttered by Mikhail Kalatozov, one-time documentarian director of *Salt for Svanetia*.

Those who embraced the poetic tendency favored emotionally open dialogue with the viewer and 'maximally capacious' [*predel'no emkie*] artistic generalizations. They fostered sharp and self-consciously artistic modes of expression. In this context, depending on directorial vision, black-and-white could symbolize moral conflict, as it does in Abuladze's *The Prayer* [Molba, 1967], or express individual authorial vision (*Ivan's Childhood*; Iuri Ilenko's *Spring for the Thirsty* [Rodnik dlia zhazhduiushhikh, 1965]. So could color, serving not as a medium of naturalistic representation of reality, but as a way of expressing a character's, or the director's, subjective apprehension of the world. Sergei Paradzhanov exploited this dimension of color's potential in his lushly beautiful *Shadows of Forgotten Ancestors* [Teni zabytykh predkov, 1964].)[41]

By the early 1960s Soviet artists and intellectuals had long since abandoned their romantic idealism of the early thaw years. A weariness with faiths of all kinds had set in, although the second stage of de-Stalinization, sparked by Khrushchev's speech at the Twenty-second Party Congress in 1961, would reanimate their hopes for a few years. Meanwhile, film-makers of both 'poetic' and 'documentary' orientation sought a cinematic form that could accommodate a less meretricious portrait of reality yet plausibly justify a happy ending; they wanted heroes who could live within the real world yet legitimately retain the innocence of an Aliosha Skvortsov, the emotional integrity of Veronika and Boris, the courage of Andrei Sokolov.

The child-protagonist provided one such hero, and at least half a dozen films appeared in 1960 and 1961 featuring children or adolescents as their protagonists. Free of the burden of Soviet history, often not even born until after Stalin's death, these children looked at the world around them with credibly wide-eyed amazement, especially the younger ones: Georgi Danelia and Igor Talankin's five-year-old protagonist Seriozha, in their 1960 film of the same name; Aliosha in Tumanov and Shchukin's *Alioshka's Love* [Aleshkina liubov', 1960]; Sandu in Mikhail Kalik's *Man Follows the Sun* [Chelovek idet za solntsem, 1961].

Compared with contemporary Western European films about children, such as Truffaut's *Four Hundred Blows* [Les Quatre cents coups, France 1959], optimism and affirmation characterize these Soviet films about children and adolescents. Even Andrei Tarkovsky, in *The Steamroller and the Violin* [Katok i skripka, 1960], the diploma film he completed at VGIK, does not explicitly reject such optimism.[42] Its heroes, seven-year-old Sasha the violinist and Sergei, the steamroller operator working on his street, become genuinely attached to each other. Forming a conventional worker–*intelligent* alliance, they learn from each other: Sergei teaches Sasha about manhood and protecting the weak, Sasha reciprocates with the power of art. (Tarkovsky tried to hire Urusevsky to film *Steamroller*, an amazingly brash act for a total novice.)[43]

But the reign of the legitimately innocent hero (whether child or eccentric, *chudak*) could not endure for long; nature dictates that children grow up. By the time Tarkovsky turned to *Ivan's Childhood*, taking over from another director, he subverted more than he accepted of Soviet tradition in fashioning his protagonist. Literary and film recreations of the Civil War frequently featured the child who 'hid the wounded commissar in the loft and dreamed of serving in Budionny's regiment'. Twenty years later, he metamorphosed into the bright, brave orphan who acted as liaison for a partisan unit, or the schoolboy, 'son of the regiment, in a fine soldier's shirt and boots'.[44] In *Fate of a Man*, for instance, Vania's guileless questions and limpet-like attachment to Sokolov had viewers brushing away tears in ready sympathy. Khutsiev's Little Fiodor is less innocent than Vania, but his brash veneer hides an emotional hunger apparent when he clings to Big Fiodor in his sleep, and when he watches the excavation of a

buried Soviet tank, a coffin for Soviet soldiers like his own father.
Several years older than Vania and Fiodor, and played not by the 'cute' child originally cast but by the formidable Kolia Burliaev, Tarkovsky's Ivan has witnessed his childhood blasted into smithereens by the Nazis. He is hardly a child at all, except in his dreams. During the first extended sequence in the dugout Ivan behaves with more composure and gravity than most of the adults in the film display. He adamantly insists that Lt Galtsev contact HQ, he concentrates single-mindedly as writes up his report on German troop strength, he sips his tea wearily and breaks off a few crumbs of bread slowly, he sleeps warily. The first childlike behavior he exhibits is a flying leap into the arms of Captain Kholin when Kholin enters the dugout, and its unexpectedness shocks us into the realization that Ivan is, after all, a child.

In the film's 'waking' reality Ivan combines physical immaturity (the pre-puberty bodily contours and child's soft skin) and frailty (ribs that are clearly visible when he strips) with a most unchildlike ferocity and self-assurance. The result is not far from frightening. Thanks principally to the dream sequences, we watch him with hearts pinched with pity, but horror accompanies the pity, not just at what this child has lost but at what he has become: the embodiment of his hatred.

Hatred defines his life and makes survival desirable. All other Soviet film heroes wish to survive: Bondarchuk's Sokolov, despite the inhumanity of the concentration camp, does whatever he must in order to endure, sustained by thoughts of his family; the exhausted and concussed soldier Iamshchikov, in Alov and Naumov's *Peace to Him Who Enters*, musters the strength to smile at the sight of a newborn infant, herald of peace. Only Ivan, godson to Veronika in *Cranes*, does not care whether he lives or dies, an indifference all the more appalling because of his age. Ivan endures because of his hatred: death would deprive him of the opportunity for vengeance. As Jean-Paul Sartre wrote, 'Surrounded by people of peace, who are willing to die for the sake of peace and to fight a war for its sake, this militant and mad child fights a war for the sake of war. He lives for that alone.'[45] We learn of his execution – recorded in the Gestapo files the Red Army discovers upon entering Berlin – with a sense not of surprise but of destiny fulfilled.

The hatred-driven Ivan undermines one commonplace of thaw

art, the innocent child-hero. Tarkovsky disrupts another, the adoption motif. Conventionally both child and adult need the relationship as emotional compensation and healing for the traumatic losses inflicted by the war. They save each other, the way Veronika and Borka do. (Even films set years after the end of the war, such as Lev Kulidzhanov's *When the Trees were Big* [Kogda derev'ia byli bol'shimi, 1961], rely on this formula.)

Tarkovsky, however, tells the story of an unsuccessful adoption. Ivan cannot be saved. None of the adults, from solidly paternal Katasonych to charming but feckless Kholin, can protect Ivan. Moreover, though they love him, they are reluctantly compelled to exploit the advantages of his age and size for their own military purposes. Before the final fantasy sequence, inserted documentary footage – including a row of small corpses, Goebbels's poisoned children – marks the 'suicide' of fascism and suggests the twin motifs of vengeance and of ravaged childhood. Not only our Ivan (and his Russian peers) have lost their childhoods to war: all children have.[46]

Ivan's Childhood depicts the war without battle scenes, by 1962 hardly an innovation in Soviet films. The entire action occurs in the interstice between two scouting missions, neither at the front nor in the rear; it takes place in the no-man's-land between and beneath them. Here Tarkovsky borrows heavily from Urusevsky, emphasising the limbo-status of the stagnant icy water Ivan must traverse to reach the dugout at the start of the film, and again toward the end, when Kholin and Galtsev row him out for another mission.

Urusevsky had given visual form to the paradox of 'unnatural' nature in *Cranes are Flying*, as Boris trudges through dead swampland and barren trees before dying amid the circling image of living birch trees, and again in the 'evil' sun of *Unsent Letter*.[47] Vadim Iusov, Tarkovsky's cameraman for *Ivan*, 'significantly expand[ed] the stylistic experimentation' of Kalatozov and Urusevsky, 'while harking back, like them, to the exploration in montage and *mise-en-scène* of the 1920s'.[48] The layering of sound as the young Red Army scout Ivan picks his way through the swamp, the dead water of the swamp itself, the filming of landscape as an element of emotional and symbolic significance rather than neutral background: all these derive at least in part from the *provody* sequence and Boris's death scene in *Cranes*.

Tarkovsky's choice of black-and-white, though partly dictated by budgetary constraints, also echoed Urusevsky's substantiation of black-and-white as a choice for a modern film: Urusevsky had persuaded viewers that black-and-white was the only choice possible for *Cranes*.[49] *Cranes* exemplified the double-edged significance of black-and-white in Soviet films of the late 1950s and well into the 1960s. At the beginning of the 1950s, and despite the high cost of color stock, film-makers began consistently to replace black-and-white with color stock (often of inferior quality) in movies of all genres – historical epics, literary adaptations and children's movies. Color films occupied the highest rung on the hierarchy of planning and production, and the authorities rewarded film-makers who responded appropriately to official mandates, called *sotsial'nyi zakaz* in Soviet parlance, with color stock. (The most privileged had access to expensive imported Kodachrome stock.)

Oddly, perhaps as a legacy from newsreels, black-and-white affirmed the veracity and naturalness of what was represented on screen, even though it lacked one of the most important characteristics of objective reality, color. Thus when film-makers – veterans and novices alike – sought verisimilitude as an ideal of the early thaw years, they chose black-and-white, in part as a reaction against the pomposity and officially mandated 'high style', literally rose-colored, of the color films of the late Stalin years. For Kalatozov and Urusevsky, as for others in that early period, black-and-white seemed *a priori* to signify reliability and truthfulness.[50] Although Kalatozov and Urusevsky differed from many of their colleagues in their deliberately obtrusive and romantic visual style, they too preferred black-and-white for their intense, dynamic, careful observation of their heroes, their environment, their psychology.

Tarkovsky and Iusov go beyond Kalatozov and Urusevsky. In *Ivan* war deforms nature but it also capitalizes on nature's components, the building blocks for war. The trees of Ivan's dreams become the stumps of waking reality. War wrenches the 'preternaturally mature and ... eerily intense'[51] boy-soldier out of the world of nature to which he organically belongs, the world of sunlight and apples, goats and horses, where he follows a butterfly through the air and listens entranced to the cuckoo. He must use his knowledge of that world, now rendered a stagnant world of lifeless nature, to help the war effort. The landscape is less external than internal, Ivan's blasted interior world.[52]

The original script for *Ivan's Childhood* ended with affirmation: Ivan survives and Galtsev utters the last words of the film, 'Blessed be peace.'[53] But Tarkovsky filmed something else: complete emotional devastation. Chaliapin's song on the gramophone, itself about incomplete love ('Masha isn't led across the river' – in other words, cannot marry), breaks off. The living birch trees in the curious scene between the nurse Masha and Kholin contrast with their abortive and unsuccessful attempt to come together. In Tarkovsky's film, war blights or stunts every form of love, reduces passion to Masha's anesthetized passivity, truncates paternal concern, eviscerates filial and familial love or inverts it into hatred.

Tarkovsky revised the narrative of the original novella, where Ivan's 'story' is told from the outside, without embellishment, by young Lieutenant Galtsev.[54] By shifting the point of view and by adding the extremely powerful dream sequences, Tarkovsky penetrates Ivan's consciousness and creates a new and purely cinematic linkage within and organization of his material.[55] Uniting emotion and reason via the 'logic of associative links,' he offers a vision thematically and aesthetically distant from 'poetic' films such as *Man Follows the Sun*, on the one hand, and from 'prosaic' films such as *And What If It's Love?*, on the other.

Yet just as Tarkovsky combined and revised multiple thematic elements characteristic of the thaw in *Ivan's Childhood* – the child at its center, the surrogate parenting, the primacy of emotions – so, too, he 'borrowed' many of the component devices of *Ivan's Childhood*. Romm used interior monologue in *Nine Days*. Kalatozov deployed fantasy in *Cranes*. Kalik and Chukhrai turned their cameras upside down, and several film-makers incorporated documentary footage. In that sense, for all his immense originality, Tarkovsky's artistic choices emerged from his context and era no less than did his thematic preoccupations. For Tarkovsky, as for so many of his generation of film writers, cinematographers and directors, *The Cranes are Flying* epitomized individual artistic vision; it became a liberating paradigm thanks to which he, and dozens of others like him, took the risk of trusting their own judgments and their own artistic visions.

Notes

1. Sergei Gerasimov, 'Razmyshleniia o molodykh', *Iskusstvo kino* 2 (1960), p. 18.
2. Ibid., pp. 21–2.
3. D. Pisarevskii, 'Vtoraia zhizn' literaturnogo obraza', abridged transcript of discussion held at the Academy of Sciences, *Iskusstvo kino* 6 (1959), p. 88.
4. Ia. Varshavskii, 'Potrebnost' molodoi dushi', *Iskusstvo kino* 10 (1960), p. 31. He cites a studio administrator who accused *Ballad of a Soldier* of 'pathology' because Shura cries out in alarm when – thinking herself alone in the box car of the train – she spies Aliosha. 'Why did she cry out? It wasn't a fascist soldier she saw, after all' (pp. 31–2).
5. I. Shneiderman, 'Ballada o soldate', in *Molodye rezhissery sovetskogo kino* (Moscow, 1962), pp. 108–9.
6. S. Rostotskii, 'Ot imeni pokoleniia', *Iskusstvo kino* 1 (1960), pp. 66–7.
7. E. Vorob'ev, 'Ia vam zhit' zaveshchaiu', *Iskusstvo kino* 1 (1960), p. 70.
8. Zakhar Agranenko, 'S liubov'iu k geroiu-rovesniku', and Nina Ignat'eva, 'Èto nuzhno liudiam', *Iskusstvo kino* 1 (1960).
9. Cited by Lev Anninskii, *Shestidesiatniki i my* (Moscow, 1991), p. 46. The film took many Soviet prizes in 1960 and 1961 (including a Lenin Prize for Chukhrai and his co-author Valentin Ezhov), as well as Grand Prizes at 1960 Czech, San Francisco and Polish festivals, and other awards in London, Milan, Mexico, Tehran, Athens.
10. Maia Turovskaia, 'Ballada o soldate', *Novyi mir* 4 (1961), p. 250.
11. Valerii Fomin, *Vse kraski siuzheta* (Moscow, 1971), pp. 65–6.
12. Anninskii, *Shestidesiatniki* ... , pp. 47–8. Julian Graffy notes that the film-makers portray Liza with an element of sympathy and understanding, despite her infidelity – compassion perhaps learned from *Cranes*.
13. Fomin, *Vse kraski* ... , p. 70.
14. Marlen Khutsiev, 'Ia nikogda ne delal polemichnykh fil'mov', in V. Troianovskii (ed.), *Kinematograf ottepeli* (Moscow, 1996), p. 195.
15. Cited by Miron Chernenko, *Marlen Khutsiev: Tvorcheskii portret* (Moscow, 1988), p. 10. The film, incidentally, is in black-and-white.
16. Neia Zorkaia, 'O iasnosti tseli', *Iskusstvo kino* 4 (1959), p. 39.
17. Maia Turovskaia, 'Kharakter i vremia', *Iskusstvo kino* 4 (1959), p. 24.
18. Viktor Nekrasov, 'Slova "velikie" i "prostye"', *Iskusstvo kino* 5 (1959), p. 58.
19. Ia. Varshavskii, 'Nado razobrat'sia', *Iskusstvo kino* 5 (1959), pp. 62–3.
20. A. Karaganov, 'Geroi nashikh dnei', *Iskusstvo kino* 7 (1959), p. 42.
21. Vadim Baskakov, *Spor prodolzhaetsia* (Moscow, 1968); cited in L. N. Poznanskaia (ed.), *Letiat zhuravli* (Moscow, 1972), p. 134.
22. Mikhail Kuznetsov, *Geroi nashikh fil'mov* (Moscow, 1965), p. 59.

23. V. Iusov, 'Predannost' prizvaniiu', *Iskusstvo kino* 3 (1980), p. 100.
24. Cited by Iurii Bogomolov, *Mikhail Kalatozov: Stranitsy tvorcheskoi biografii* (Moscow, 1989), p. 162.
25. V. Goriaev, 'Prostranstvo Urusevskogo', *Iskusstvo kino* 3 (1980), p. 83.
26. Cited in Poznanskaia (ed.), *Letiat zhuravli*, p. 133, from *Èkran i tip* (Moscow, 1966).
27. Semen Freilikh, 'Proshloe i budushchee', in Poznanskaia (ed.), *Letiat zhuravli*, p. 7.
28. German Kremlev, *Mikhail Kalatozov* (Moscow, 1964), p. 204.
29. Anninskii, *Shestidesiatniki* ... , pp. 58–9. Shpalikov's hero in *A Long and Happy Life*, striking up a friendship with a pretty girl on a bus, mockingly recites the words to identify himself.
30. Kremlev, *Mikhail Kalatozov*, p. 215.
31. Cited in ibid., p. 226.
32. Anninskii, *Shestidesiatniki* ... , p. 61.
33. Evgenii Margolit, 'Peizazh s geroem', in V. Troianovskii (ed.), *Kinematograf ottepeli*, p. 108.
34. Valentin Liukov and Iurii Panov, 'Èto li gorizonty?', *Oktiabr'* 5 (1962), pp. 184–5.
35. Marlen Khutsiev, interview, Tatiana Khopliankina, *Zastava Il'icha: sud'ba fil'ma* (Moscow, 1990), p. 31.
36. Ibid., pp. 36–7.
37. Bogomolov, *Mikhail Kalatozov*, p. 188.
38. Irina Shilova, 'Cherno-beloe kino', *Kinovedcheskie zapiski* 32 (1996–97), p. 31.
39. Evgenii Margolit, *Sovetskoe kinoiskusstvo. Osnovnye ètapy stanovleniia i razvitiia* (Moscow, 1988), p. 77.
40. Cited by Valerii Fomin, 'Mezhdu poeziei i prozoi', in V. Fomin (ed.), *Kinopanorama: Sovetskoe kino segodnia. Sbornik statei* (Moscow, 1974), p. 111.
41. Margolit, *Sovetskoe kinoiskusstvo*, pp. 82–3.
42. 'Colour, Soviet "reality", Soviet rhetoric and sentimentality would all be banished from the later films, the last three never to return.' Julian Graffy, 'Tarkovsky: The Weight of the World', *Sight and Sound*, January 1997, p. 20.
43. Vida Johnson and Graham Petrie, *The Films of Andrei Tarkovsky* (Bloomington, IN, 1994), p. 63.
44. Neia Zorkaia, 'Chernoe derevo u reki', *Iskusstvo kino* 7 (1962), p. 103.
45. Jean-Paul Sartre, 'Po povodu *Ivanova detstva*', *Mir i fil'my Andreia Tarkovskogo* (Moscow, 1991), p. 14. Originally published in *L'Unità*, 9 October 1963, reprinted in *Les Lettres françaises*, 26 December 1963–1 January 1964.

46. Maia Turovskaia, 'Prozaicheskoe i poèticheskoe kino segodnia', *Novyi mir* 9 (1962), p. 250, and Denise Youngblood, 'Post-Stalinist Cinema and the Myth of World War II: Tarkovskii's *Ivan's Childhood* (1962) and Klimov's *Come and See* (1985)', *Historical Journal of Film, Radio and Television* 14, 4 (1994), p. 416.
47. Turovskaia notes the multiple connotations of the image of the sun, from Sholokhov's 'black sun' when Gregor buries Aksinia, to the sun in the medieval 'Lay of Prince Igor'. 'Prozaicheskoe i poèticheskoe kino segodnia,' p. 249.
48. Johnson and Petrie, *The Films* ... , p. 14.
49. A. Shelenkov, cited in Poznanskaia (ed.), *Letiat zhuravli*, p. 137.
50. Shilova, 'Cherno-beloe kino', p. 25.
51. Youngblood, 'Post-Stalinist Cinema ... ', p. 415.
52. Evgenii Margolit, 'Peizazh s geroem', in Troianovskii (ed.), *Kinematograf ottepeli*, p. 110.
53. Neia Zorkaia, 'Nachalo', in *Mir i fil'my Andreia Tarkovskogo*, p. 31.
54. For comparisons with the Bogomolov text, see Zorkaia, 'Chernoe derevo u reki', pp. 104–5; Turovskaia, 'Prozaicheskoe i poèticheskoe kino segodnia', pp. 248–9; Anninskii, *Shestidesiatniki i my*, pp. 108–9.
55. See Fomin, *Vse kraski siuzheta*, pp. 72–6, and A. Nekhoroshev, *Techenie fil'ma: o kinematograficheskom siuzhete* (Moscow, 1975), pp. 55–70 passim.

6. Conclusion

Soviet audiences never entirely forgot *Cranes*, nor did film-makers. But for two generations of both Russian and Western critics and fans, *Cranes* receded into the background of their consciousness, only to re-emerge in the past fifteen years as a central symbol of the thaw, its actors and images as instantly evocative of a time and mood as, say, Chaplin's feeding machine or the arches of Rick's bar in *Casablanca*.

A leading Russian film journal, *Kinovedcheskie zapiski*, published four pieces about the film in 1993. Three essays in *Cinema of the Thaw* [Kinematograf ottepeli, 1996], the first major book by Russian scholars on this subject, pay special attention to *Cranes*, and the volume's editor chose stills of Boris and Veronika to adorn the front and back covers, so that only the book's spine separates their embrace. In November 2000 a program entitled 'Soviet Cinema of the 1960s' ran for three weeks at New York's Lincoln Center, and subsequently travelled around the United States. The full group of twenty-five movies included *Cranes*, though *Cranes* dates from 1957, and the series brochure placed Veronika's image on its cover: her face, unobscured by the words superimposed at the top and bottom, takes up the full page.

Such prominence suggests the significance of *Cranes* even now, and even for viewers too young to have seen the film when it opened. The Brezhnev era, with its intolerance toward political, national and cultural independence and dissidence, stifled many of the hopes and possibilities heralded by the thaw. The men and women who came of age in the late 1950s and 1960s had professional and personal battles to fight between 1968 and 1986, battles to which *Cranes* was not germane. The film-makers among them were trying to get their own scripts approved, their own movies on to screens, while film critics found *Cranes* too recent for any kind of long perspective, and in any event could not realistically hope for censorship approval with manuscripts about the thaw.[1]

Mikhail Gorbachev, with his twinned policies of *perestroika* and *glasnost*, rekindled many of the aspirations closeted or suspended for more than twenty years. Indeed, he relied upon the help of liberals from the 1960s, 'Khrushchev's children', the so-called *shestidesiatniki*, by the mid-1980s men and women mostly in their sixties. They turned back to *Cranes*, as they turned back to many other achievements of the Khrushchev era, with a mixture of nostalgia and understandable pride, as an emblem of their youth, when the nation's problems seemed soluble, given enlightened political leadership, flexibility and a return to what many of them perceived as a kind of early-Bolshevik idealism. Their own children, now in their thirties and forties, have trained a more detached and professional eye on *Cranes*, understanding it as a film crucial to the evolution of Soviet film art in subsequent decades, as well as an essential part of their cultural history with links to earlier as well as later Soviet cinema.

'It all began with *Cranes*,' wrote Lev Anninsky. '*Cranes* marked a turn in the road.'[2] Anninsky's ringing – hyperbolic? – assertions conceal at least two salient questions. First of all, *what* exactly 'began' with *Cranes*? 'Turn' signals a marked change of direction: from what, towards what? Second, since Anninsky's 'it' implies not simply a cinematic transformation, but something supra-cinematic, a social or cultural process, how could a movie have that much resonance? How could any movie, however good, affect its audiences in their lives outside the movie theater? Trying to formulate answers to these two questions seems an appropriate way to conclude a book on *The Cranes are Flying*.

The 'What'

The first question is slightly more straightforward than the second. Anninsky's 'it' cannot refer to the thaw in general, since the thaw had its roots in politics and economics as much as, if not more than, in culture, and since it began several years before *The Cranes are Flying* opened. Almost as soon as Stalin died in March 1953 the Soviet Union began to change, if at first in tiny and barely perceptible ways. Khrushchev's revelatory peroration on the final day of the Twentieth Party Congress in February 1956, despite its supposedly restricted audience, markedly accelerated the metamorphosis of Soviet society.

The thaw took many detours. Hesitations and backsliding marked it no less than did liberalization and greater candor; skittish compromises and dogmatic retrenchments hobbled almost every step forward. And cinema, as part of the Soviet Union's cultural machinery and as an industry dependent upon Party support and state subsidies, necessarily reacted to mutations and modulations in official policy. When an ill wind blew from the Kremlin, as it often enough did, the cinema establishment shied nervously, recoiled, sometimes retreated.

Nevertheless, by and large the thaw did make headway, and the straitjacket that had confined Soviet culture and society loosened. Like other arts, cinema both enjoyed and on occasion forced an expansion of those opportunities. In the middle and late 1950s, film-makers reconsidered such fundamental concepts as the nature of heroism and the role of family, reconfigured the relationship of private life to the public domain, revised key aspects of national history. Film-makers reassessed patterns dominant during the culture of the Stalin era, especially the last years that were so disastrous for cinema: the deified leader, the evaporation of ordinary men and women from the screen, inexorable optimism and no less importunate intolerance of any doubt or ambiguity.

The new movies legitimated private emotions, the prosaic, even mundane, lives of fallible, puzzled and ambivalent human beings. Scriptwriters devised slightly more than two-, if not yet three-dimensional villains, instead of the caricatures of the past. Directors tried hard to avoid the bogus, and to achieve a measure of authenticity and veracity – though official constraints continued to calculate and circumscribe that measure – in their portraits of Soviet life. They portrayed crucial and mythologized national icons – Lenin, the Bolshevik Revolution, the collective farms, the Young Communist League, the Civil War and the Second World War – with different emphases, and from different angles, than had been possible before. By 1957, when *Cranes* opened, a substantial number of writers and dramatists, and a smaller but appreciable number of film-makers, had already exploited every discernible crack in the official façade to treat their subjects and develop their themes honestly. In all these respects *The Cranes are Flying* capitalized on its many predecessors, representing another stage in Soviet society's slow, long and often tortuous process of emancipation from its Stalinist legacy. Thus *Cranes* gave viewers the Second World War as most of them had experienced it, far from the front – war in terms of waiting and worrying, of widow- and orphanhood, of physical disruption and psychological anxiety. It characterized its primary villain, Mark, chiefly as a weak and corruptible man, easier to disdain than to detest. Mark's heroic counterpart, Boris, lacks many (though not all) of the attributes conventionally associated with Soviet screen heroes, and in any event disappears halfway through the film. Boris's father, Fiodor Ivanovich, is a figure of pathos as well as a sagacious authority. After such a long period of cinematic fatherlessness, to have a wise and sustaining but also human and credible father figure as the center of the family is itself remarkable, and Fiodor Ivanovich's unimpeachable moral prestige underscores the truth of his sallies against the debasing effect of ubiquitous Soviet bombast.

In these areas *Cranes* continued, extended and elaborated trends already discernible in movies like *A Person is Born*, *Soldiers*, *Pavel Korchagin* and *Spring on Zarechnaia Street*. But *Cranes* did not simply expand existing propensities. The organizers of the Lincoln Center program properly incorporated *Cranes* in their retrospective of Soviet films from the 1960s, because the films that followed *Cranes* would not have been made as they were, had *Cranes* not preceded them. In three key respects it charted unknown territory, and paved the way for future films. Its radicalism consisted, first, of the character of Veronika; second, of the film-makers' judgment of Veronika; and third, of the manner in which they chose to film their movie.

What makes Veronika such an innovation? First and foremost, the contradiction between her action – betrayal – and what can perhaps best be called her essence. Indifferent to and independent from the social and societal dimensions of life, she exists for and embodies love. Love defines her autonomy and gives her life meaning. She betrays that love when she marries Mark. Yet though she breaks faith, she never forsakes it: her love proves far more enduring than

Conclusion 107

her disloyalty. Her guilt and self-punishment, her misery and her inability to believe in Boris's death do not simply expiate the betrayal, they constitute her way of remaining true to herself. And when she hears Boris's voice reading the note hidden under the gold nuts of the toy squirrel's basket, she hears the voice of love acknowledging and recognizing her fundamental, abiding fidelity. The paradox of Veronika, with its primacy of emotion over logic and reason, had no forerunner – and relatively few successors – on the Soviet screen.

Second, Kalatozov and Urusevsky tossed this puzzle at their audience with virtually no indication of their own views, and no guidelines on how that audience 'should' react. It is true that Samoilova's exceptional appeal, Urusevsky's empathetic camera, and Fiodor Ivanovich's clemency combine to invite our own compassion and sympathy for Veronika. At the same time, the film quite deliberately eschews explaining Veronika's decision to marry Mark: Kalatozov leaves it a mystery, for us to unravel or not as best we can.

By doing so they flouted Soviet tradition, which expected and endorsed much more explicit authorial judgment than Kalatozov and Urusevsky supply. *Cranes* proffers no easily-applied labels, no facile categories, no glib verdicts. (Chukhrai, by contrast, provided a voice-over narrator for *Ballad of a Soldier* who more or less tells the audience what to think.) In this regard, while *Cranes* had antecedents, it took a big risk, because it eschewed judgment in a particularly sensitive and iconic domain: a woman's loyalty to a soldier fighting a desperate war. Kalatozov's trust in his audience, his refusal to create yet another edifying parable, freed other film-makers to do the same.

Finally, the cinematic language of *Cranes*. Critics both at home and abroad immediately discerned connections between the lyricism and fluidity of Urusevsky's camerawork and the great films of the Soviet silent era, and rightly so. Kalatozov and Urusevsky's visual vocabulary – the extreme low- and high-angle shots, symbolic *mise-en-scène*, expressive dollying and panning – owes much to Eisenstein, Pudovkin and Dovzhenko, as well as to Kalatozov's own early work in *Salt for Svanetia*. The Soviet critical establishment of the Stalin years, conforming to Party discipline, had long repudiated such expressive means as 'formalism', had joined official condemnation of individual style and innovation in favor of a bland, static and undifferentiated middle-brow monotony.

By 1957 Khutsiev, Chukhrai, Vasili Ordynsky, Alov and Naumov and others had shrugged off that inhibiting shroud, had ventured into considerably more imaginative cinematography. Nevertheless, *Cranes* heralded a startling originality of visual design and movement. Urusevsky's earlier work in the 1950s films, especially for Chukhrai in *The Forty-first*, hinted at that freedom, but in *Cranes* it developed to an unparalleled degree. Only these specific artists, with their unique vision, could have made this particular movie.

The artistic sovereignty inherent in and validated by *Cranes* influenced Soviet film-makers for the next twenty years. In the 1960s directors like Ioseliani, Tarkovsky, Paradzhanov, Muratova, Shepitko, Riazanov, Klimov, Panfilov and Smirnov, each devising his or her own means, attempted to replicate that sovereignty. All of them aspired to freshen audience perception, to force spectators out of their accustomed perception and to create free zones of consciousness untrammeled by the blinkers of convention, of expectation, of ideology. Few of those directors borrowed the specific visual style of *Cranes*. But they all emulated Kalatozov and Urusevsky's independence, their refusal to compromise.

The 'Why'

The second question embedded in Anninsky's resounding declaration pertains to the impact of *Cranes*. Its repercussions and reverberations far transcended – he implied – the confines of the movie theater. One can discount the overstatement of his assessment, but not the basic judgment, which is borne out by documents, by memoirs and by memories. The reasons that a movie could have such an effect go beyond film analysis to impinge on sociology, history, psychology.

Anninsky himself identified three segments of *Cranes*' domestic audiences as soldiers who had fought at the front; widows – 'our lonely mothers' – whose lives had been so filled with cares, during and after the war years, that they had never had a moment to think about themselves; and young people ready to grapple with the significance of their own early childhoods, often deprived of paternal presence, guidance and love. *Cranes* compelled all three groups first to respond to the film's emotional demands and then to ponder the war and their own experiences in and because of it. The film made them consider why they had become what they were.[3]

And they did. When they argued about Veronika, about trust, they were arguing about their own behavior, or their parents'. The film, with its validation of the supremacy of feeling, presented them with a compelling alternative to officially enshrined values. Its definition of love, owing nothing to the public domain, to civic obligation, to satisfactions of service, won over its audiences, especially its young audiences. To find a woman like Veronika, to *be* a woman like Veronika – these became goals, or fantasies, for millions of young Soviet men and women.

Cranes' impact owed much to the undoubted popularity of movies in the Soviet Union throughout the 1950s and indeed well into the 1960s. Surveys found that the average Soviet citizen in those years visited movie theaters at least twice a month; regular viewers attended movie theaters about thirty-five times a year. In other words, people spent about as much time at the movies as they spent reading newspapers. Until the late 1960s, when television displaced cinema as the dominant medium of entertainment and information, cinema occupied pride of place among the arts in influencing how people dressed and combed their hair, the songs they sang, the music they danced to, the pictures they hung on their walls. It shaped what they yearned for, and affected how they understood their history and construed their possibilities. Formal ideology, Marxist-Leninist and Socialist Realist, retained its official dominance; like any revealed truth, it excluded significant modification. But slippery and amorphous cultural paradigms could and did change. With *The Cranes are Flying*, cinema – in its power to affect viewers, to impress on them new images, to manipulate how as well as what they saw – may finally have merited the famous description attributed to Lenin, as the most important of all the arts.

Notes

1. Lev Anninskii wrote his study of cinema in 1967, considering it at the time a book about contemporary cinema. The book, entitled *Men of the '60s and Us* [Shestidesiatniki i my], appeared in print in Moscow in 1991.
2. Ibid., pp. 8, 10.
3. Ibid., pp. 9.

Further Reading

Brumberg, Abraham (ed.), *Russia Under Khrushchev*, New York, 1962
C., K., *BFI Monthly Film Bulletin*, October 1958, p. 125
Candor, Rex, 'Cannes 1958', *Films in Review*, IX (6) June–July 1958, pp. 290–5
Crowther, Bosley, 'The Cranes are Flying', *New York Times*, 22 March 1960, 31: 2
Leyda, Jay, *Kino: A History of the Russian and Soviet Film*, London and Princeton, NJ, 1960
Liehm, M. and A., *The Most Important Art: Soviet and East European Film After 1945*, Berkeley, CA, 1977
Lifton, Mitchell, '*The Cranes are Flying*', *Film Quarterly* xiii (3), Spring 1960
Navailh, Françoise, '*Quand passent les cigognes*: Histoire d'un malentendu', *De Russie et Ailleurs*, Paris, 1995
Rothberg, Abraham, *The Heirs of Stalin: Dissidence and the Soviet Regime, 1953–1970*, Ithaca NY and London, 1972
Shrayer, Maxim, 'Why are the Cranes Still Flying?', *Russian Review* 56 (July 1997)
Stites, Richard, *Russian Popular Culture: Entertainment and Society since 1900*, Cambridge, 1992
Woll, Josephine, *Real Images: Soviet Cinema and the Thaw*, London and New York, 2000
Zorkaya, Neya, *The Illustrated History of Soviet Cinema*, New York, 1989

Reviews of the film appeared in *Commonweal* (18 December 1959), *The Nation* (9 April 1960), *New Yorker* (2 April 1960), *Newsweek* (7 December 1959) and *Time* (22 February 1960).

In Russian

Anninskii, Lev, *Shestidesiatniki i my* [Men of the '60s and Us], Moscow, 1991

Bogomolov, Iurii, *Mikhail Kalatozov: Stranitsy tvorcheskoi biografii*, Moscow, 1989

Kremlev, German, *Mikhail Kalatozov*, Moscow, 1964

Poznanskaia L.N. (ed.), *Letiat zhuravli* [The Cranes are Flying], Moscow, 1972

Troianovskii,Vitalii, (ed.), *Kinematograf ottepeli* [The Cinema of the Thaw], Moscow, 1996